A Gaudy Spree

Samuel Marx

A GAUDY SPREE

The Literary Life
of Hollywood
in the 1930s
When the West
Was Fun

FRANKLIN WATTS   NEW YORK   TORONTO   1987

Library of Congress Cataloging-in-Publication Data

Marx, Samuel, 1902–
A gaudy spree.

Includes index.
1. Marx, Samuel, 1902– . 2. Story editors
(Motion pictures)—California—Los Angeles—Biography.
3. Moving-picture industry—California—Los Angeles.
4. Hollywood (Los Angeles, Calif.)—Social life and
customs. I. Title.

PN1998.A3M323165   1987   791.43′092′4   [B]   86-32434
ISBN 0-531-15008-9

A Gaudy Spree

Foreword

It took a half-century to put this viewpoint in focus but, if one concedes that screen writing is a form of art, experts say we gain our best perspective of art by standing away from it. Here, then, are Hollywood authors and the fun of making movies seen from a distance of fifty years.

This flashback took shape when a publisher asked Thomas Quinn Curtiss for a book on the best writers of the first talking pictures. Mr. Curtiss, an excellent biographer who also covers the European entertainment field for the *International Herald Tribune* and *Variety,* suggested I do it.

The 1930s were memorable years. California's second gold rush was on. Hollywood was the mother lode. They crossed the continent not in covered wagons but in Pullmans. The cry was "Dialogue!" and instead of looking for it, they brought it with them. The words they carried west could be sold for gold.

A pioneer celebrant at this feast, Herman Mankiewicz, telegraphed his friend Ben Hecht in Chicago: MILLIONS ARE TO BE GRABBED OUT HERE AND YOUR ONLY COMPETITION IS IDIOTS. Then he added a thoughtful postscript: DON'T LET THIS GET AROUND.

Inadvertently, many chroniclers of that era have twisted details, misquoted what was said, attributed lines to the wrong person. I was lucky to be an eye-and-ear witness, an impressionable wanderer with a memory like an expanding universe. I have sought in this book to set Hollywood history straight.

I wish to thank Tom Curtiss for inspiring this book, Marianne Klein for the subtitle *When the West Was Fun,* and F. Scott Fitzgerald for writing "There seems little doubt about what was going to happen—America was going on the greatest, gaudiest spree in history and there was going to be plenty to tell about it."

My sentiments, exactly.

Samuel Marx

Chapter One

This Gaudy Spree began New Year's Eve, December 31, 1929, in the big, boisterous city of New York. It was an improbable time for a party. Dark shadows of depression were encircling the world in the wake of the Wall Street crash. The curtain was descending on the Roaring Twenties.

The accepted custom was for restaurant owners to hike New Year's Eve prices as high as they could count. But not at The Tavern on Forty-eighth Street, a few steps from Broadway. There, proprietor Billy LaHiff closed his doors to the public and invited a crowd of characters whose company he enjoyed and who weren't inclined to pay, anyway. Food, drink, and celebration were on the house. It was the perfect way to party.

My wife Marie and I sat at a table with an assortment of literate adults in silly hats, polluting the night air with nerve-jangling horns and noisemakers. The bedlam peaked at midnight and when it subsided I imprudently announced that we would soon depart for California, Southern California, to be exact. To be precise, we were heading for Hollywood.

I should have known better. No matter where they were born, this bunch of free-loading journalists were all New Yorkers now, and, at the moment, quite drunk.

I shouldn't have mentioned anywhere on the wrong side of the Hudson River to these erudite sophisticates who loved New York City. My announcement triggered a fusillade of scorn.

Damon Runyon had a soft, kindly voice and gave the impression of a fatherly figure in whom you could confide the secrets of your life. He reminded us that Hollywood was Bridgeport with palms and we should be alert to its deceptive elements.

"Stay away from earthquakes, kids. That's an order!"

"Southern California," mused Jack Lait. "The Bellyache Belt of America." Lait was an expert at creating slangy phrases for *Variety*, the theatrical bible. "The joint is jumping with foreigners from Arkansas and Missouri. They set brush fires and barbecue New Yorkers on them."

"They'll tell you it never rains in ol' Californy," drawled columnist Mark Hellinger. "Then you drown crossing the street. They use the sun as an overhead sewer system."

"Their envy is showing," I told Marie. "Tomorrow they'll call to see if they can hitch a ride."

In the taxi on our way to our uptown apartment, she said their remarks hadn't dampened her enthusiasm for the trip.

"They were trying out lines to use in the pieces they write," she said. "Just like you do."

It was dawn and the streets of my old home town were empty and quiet. A new year always gave birth to thoughtful contemplation, reflections on the outgoing, hopes for the incoming. This was more than a new year, it was a new decade. That could make a difference. How great was impossible to imagine on New Year's Eve. But later, in retrospect, it was obvious that was the night the party began.

I was the contented editor, reporter, and entire writing staff of *New York Amusements,* a weekly periodical that detailed the varied entertainments available through the metropolis. It was dispensed free on counters in hotels, barber shops, and miscellaneous gathering places. It subsisted on its advertising revenue, which see-sawed between profit and loss, depending on how often my free-wheeling writing style antagonized its advertisers. The young woman in charge of that department (the only other employee on the payroll) alternated between anger at my refusal to bend an opinion in favor of her customers and her agreement that the booklet was extremely readable and could boast of more devoted followers than any similar publication.

Covering Broadway was an enjoyable way to pass pleasant hours. There were plays to see, movies to review and celebrities to interview. The pay was adequate, enough to permit a contented bachelorhood until a cautious friendship with Marie developed into a deep and lasting love and, toward the end of the Twenties, a marriage to match.

In December 1929, a few months after we were wed, I ran into Irving Thalberg on a Manhattan side street. He had become a fabled "Boy Wonder" at making motion pictures since our acquaintanceship began. He was a minor secretary then, he now headed all production at the Metro-Goldwyn-Mayer Studio, which was steadily becoming the best in the business.

Our unexpected meeting occurred midway between my office and his hotel. We stood on West Fifty-fourth Street, not really needing to exchange the usual recounting of what had happened since we last saw each other. His preeminence in the movie industry and his marriage to film star Norma Shearer were widely publicized. He knew about me because I had thoughtfully placed his name on the mailing list of *New York Amusements*.

He asked what salary I was making and then suggested I try my hand at screen writing in Hollywood.

"See if you can get a three-month leave from your job and come anytime you like. I'll give you the same money you're getting now and if it works out I'll give you a raise. At least you'll have a vacation with pay."

It sounded reasonable enough but later some skeptic told Marie, "When they really want someone in Hollywood, they send a private railway car. They didn't even send your husband a pair of roller skates."

When she repeated it to me, she said, "Don't worry about it. Someone's always taking the joy out of life." If it worried her, she refrained from showing it to me. She had a wonderful way of riding out all the erratic turns one encounters in changing destinies.

No less a figure than Florenz Ziegfeld, Jr., the producer with the vaunted slogan "Glorifying the American Girl," had effected one of those turns in Marie's destiny when she made her first appearance in New York. It happened two years before we met.

Schooled in ballet in Boston, she intended to pursue a career as a dancer. It took months to persuade her mother that New York was the place to work at it. Finally she won her point and, immediately on her arrival, began the rounds of musical show producers.

She was pretty enough to capture the approval of the jaded female at Ziegfeld's reception desk, who marched her straight in to him. He gave Marie's legs an appreciative glance, then handed her a ticket to that evening's performance of *Sally* at the New Amsterdam Theatre, which was directly downstairs from his office.

"Come back tomorrow and let me know if you can do the dances," he told her.

She told him she could do them all, especially the fluttery toe dancing of the moths in the Butterfly Ballet. Thereupon he signed her to a fifty-dollar-a-week, run-of-the-play contract.

Finding the job she wanted so quickly was a dream come true. Only two days in New York and already a professional dancer! What luck!

Unknowingly she had shown up just as the show's long Broadway run was ending. That weekend it moved to Boston and for the next six months she was back home with mother, sleeping in her own bed. She stayed on when *Sally* toured the Pacific Coast, then came back to Broadway and me.

We set May 1 as our departure date for a leisurely month of cross-country driving and sightseeing. I wrote a note to that effect to Thalberg which, in light of his reaction to my arrival, I don't think he ever saw.

———

—6—

I would be leaving New York with the mixture of feelings that inevitably accompanies the elation of travel and the qualms of quitting familiar surroundings.

In the Spring of 1930, Manhattan presented a curious climate of contrasts. Downtown on the Bowery, there was no elation. Breadlines and soup kitchens played to standing room only. The new poor had to grab space in a flophouse before noon, like making a reservation for a hit show.

Uptown, the mood on Broadway was more buoyant. No fewer than forty-five legitimate theatres were entertaining playgoers, their balcony and gallery seats ranging from one to three dollars; better locations cost six.

Anyone with a compulsion to write, as I had, was inclined to pay more attention to the playwrights than the stars. Edward Sheldon and Margaret Ayer's *Dishonored Lady* was celebrating its hundredth performance, Preston Sturges's *Strictly Dishonorable* was shocking audiences with a striptease, and John Balderston's *Berkeley Square* captured a steady run of fans of the supernatural. Additionally, grim classics like Chekhov's *Uncle Vanya* and Turgenev's *A Month in the Country* were doing very well.

Sixteen movie palaces, recently (and reluctantly) converted to sound, operated in the Broadway area. They played to big matinees because out-of-work men, despairing of finding employment, hid from their families and the realities of the day in the fantasy world of films.

Obversely, in midtown after dark, there was escape from fantasy itself—the fantasy that alcoholic beverages could be forbidden by law.

Nightclubs flourished, although prohibition authorities raided them and padlocked them regularly. These sorties caused only mild problems for the followers of Texas Guinan, the best known of the late-night entertainers. Nightclub customers were followers in a true sense of the word. A padlocked club simply moved a few doors down the street and reopened the next night. The customers followed.

Guinan's partner was the brutish racketeer Larry Fay, who

loved having his name linked with his rowdy Mistress of Ceremonies. Padlocked clubs had to have a new name, so last night's El Fey became tomorrow night's Del Fey, but all were simply called The Guinan Club.

Entrance to these and the many speakeasies that Broadway chronicler Walter Winchell dubbed "upholstered sewers" was not too difficult, despite their barred doors. They opened wide to any respectable-appearing citizen who could identify himself, using some recognizable name like William Shakespeare or Abraham Lincoln. Texas Guinan continually opened her arms and her doors to magistrates before whom she had been hauled on recent nights, thanking them for the courtesy showed her and "her kids" before dismissing charges of violating the National Prohibition Act. She counted a multitude of municipal justices among her most devoted followers.

Visitors from out of town were more likely to frequent clubs like The Silver Slipper or Frivolity whose brightly lit electric signs were beacons drawing them to places of cover charges and uncovered dancing girls. The clubs served bootlegged liquor discreetly in teacups. Cabaret customers believed they had nothing to fear from the "hooch." Comics reassured them it was right off the boat, but then added, sotto voce, "Scraped off."

All this, along with the musical comedies by the Gershwins, Jerome Kern, Cole Porter, and Rodgers and Hart made every night a carnival. It was clear I was leaving a pleasant known for an uncertain unknown when I turned our car toward Hollywood.

As Confucius might have re-written his earlier observation to fit modern times: The longest journey begins with but a single tank of gas.

Like good tourists, Marie and I stared appreciatively at a large number of canyons, mountains and caverns, then tired of them like good city folk. We ended our drive a week earlier than scheduled, so I drove to the Metro-Goldwyn-Mayer Studio to apprise Irving Thalberg of my arrival. That was when I discovered he probably never read my letter. "What brings you to California?" he asked.

"Pardon me while I collapse," I said, dropping into the couch in his office. "I thought I was going to work for you."

He grinned, then turned serious and explained that an opening on his staff had occurred hardly an hour before.

"I was wondering where I'd find someone to take this job when they told me you were here. I think you can handle it. If you'd shown up yesterday I'd have given you an assignment and forgotten you. If you arrived tomorrow the position would be filled."

What position? He didn't say. Neither did the messenger boy who marched me down to my new office and whom I tried to pump somewhat obliquely, not wishing to appear idiotic about the work expected of me. All I got from him was the impressive information that "it's the only office in this part of the lot with a private can."

Back at our hotel, I told Marie something important had happened but I didn't know what it was. Then I called a writer I knew and when I told him the name of the man I was replacing, he said, "I'll be damned! You're the story editor!"

When Thalberg said, "It's a position I think you can handle," I had no way of knowing he was lining up a job for life, but that's what it proved to be.

My job. His life.

I was suddenly boss of five separate departments, all vital to an operation seeking to make a yearly program of fifty feature films. If, as has been said, the story is the cradle of the movie, then my hand was the one that rocked it.

A trio of women supervised three of my departments. "Supervisor" was a much-used word. It had a nicer sound than "Warden."

Research was under Nathalie Bucknall, a solidly built Russian woman reliably reported to have ridden with the Cossacks in World War I. She cracked the whip over two male assistants in a few tight corridors piled to the ceiling with dictionaries and encyclopedias while telephone inquiries came nonstop.

Edith Farrell supervised the secretarial department. Her girls were well-tested note-takers and speedy typists. Young, personable and ambitious, some of them became writers. Many attached themselves permanently to the men they were temporarily assigned to—as collaborators, housekeepers, mistresses and other things. During the years I held the reins over them, director King Vidor married two of them.

Dorothy Pratt, a lady with an incredible memory for every story in its huge files, handled the reading department. Its lounge resembled a quiet public library. In it a dozen men and women read the submissions that poured into the studio from around the world, then synopsized them as a time-saving device for harried producers, most of whom hated to read, anyway. The reader's pay was fifty dollars a week, absurdly low but hotly sought because the job offered escape from a tension-packed world, a hideaway for those who wanted to nurture their own writing efforts in peace.

It was a facade. Behind the calm of the reading department was a hotbed of frustration. Readers suffered from cerebral indigestion caused by a diet of materials they knew they could cook up better. And in time, some did, among them novelist Myron Brinig, playwright Tennessee Williams, and Lillian Hellman, who wrote all sorts of things.

Fortunately for me, I fell heir to a marvelous assistant. Kate Corbaley was a sixtyish woman whose way with the material submitted to us pumped the lifeblood of the story department.

That was the heart of my new position. Its every beat was devoted to finding the material Thalberg and his supervisor-producers needed to reach their unreachable goal. Our coverage averaged four hundred possibilities a week—books, plays, news items, magazines, original ideas—all flooding in from God's huge writing staff, slaving away twenty-four hours a day all around the world. The story department checked twenty thousand submissions a year and all of them crossed my desk. Those other departments were important arteries, but recognizing what could make a movie to be recommended to Thalberg, was the specter that now haunted my days. We were trying, in a sense, to keep up with God, whose output was obviously more than humans could handle.

To stay on top of that mountain of words was a challenge. I was sure I'd been born with a compulsion to read. To be paid to do it was a joy. However, the truly gaudy spree of the literary life of Hollywood in the '30s really spun most dizzily around the fifth segment of my job: the writers!

There were forty writers on the studio staff, half of them women. A few old-time scenarists and title writers were still hanging in there from the days of silent pictures, but they would be phased out by incoming dramatists. It was infinitely more difficult to make films that talked, so the writers were proliferating while the program was diminishing. Fifty films a year would never be realized, but the effort to make them remained throughout the decade.

Daytimes, I wrestled with the intricacies of a new milieu. Accustomed to life in an urban background, I vetoed Marie's idea of finding a house of our own, so she sought an apartment to replace our hotel rooms.

Her zealous pursuit of such quarters left her exhausted, while I returned from the studio restless and accustomed to nocturnal pleasures. That seemed like it should be fun, for Hollywood in 1930 enjoyed the reputation of being the wildest place on earth. It even exported the peculiar aura of its festive frolics: comedian Fatty Arbuckle's soiree, which ended in murder in San Francisco, and the suicide of star Olive Thomas in Paris were labeled Hollywood parties by the world press.

In spite of that, I thought the town innocent, old-fashioned and slow, a village where trolleys ran through the main stem, whose restaurants and clubs were prosaic. Neighboring Los Angeles, which I also explored, was archaic and unattractive after dark. It provoked some cynic to remark that "No matter how hot it gets in the daytime, it's always dull at night."

Some of the more absorbing news columns, printed daily, were the obituaries in the *Hollywood Citizen-News* that included in the record of every demised person "Here three years" or "Here five years" or whatever, indicating to me that nobody was born in this area. If sex was rampant, it wasn't doing much for procreation.

Within my first week at the studio, a staff writer dropped an autographed book on my desk. A handsome six-footer, Joseph Moncure March was a new name to me. He was more concerned with being a poet than a screen writer but confided that he wouldn't be averse to selling the movie rights. It was a taut grouping of harsh and explosive rhymings called *The Wild Party,* and we did, in fact, buy those rights.

Reading portions out loud to Marie, I told her we must try to be invited to the good parties.

"They'll put us in the swim," I said. "Listen to this."

> *The party began to reek of sex,*
> *White arms encircled swollen necks:*
> *Blurred faces swam together: Locked*
> > *Red hungry lips:*
> > *Closed eyes:*
> > *Rocked.*
> *White shoulders burst their ribbon bands;*
> *Rose bare to passionate, fumbling hands;*
> *White slender throats curved back beneath*
> *Attacking mouths that choked their breath.*
> > *They murmured:*
> > *They gasped:*
> *They lurched, and pawed, and grasped!*

"If someone asks us to that kind of party," she said matter-of-factly, "you go and tell me all about it."

When the booming voice of Arthur Caesar roared through our telephone with a dinner invitation, I assured her that a dinner with him would fall within her requirements. He stipulated that it would be an evening of *social* intercourse.

"Let Caesar be the first to welcome you, O tattered migrant from the concrete ghetto! Only Mighty Caesar holds high the torch of knowledge in this cultural desert!"

I promised Marie a fun evening, building up the writer's coast-to-coast reputation for one-liners, including his own assessment of his California status: "From Poland to polo in one generation!"

We arrived at Caesar's hillside home at seven, as bidden, met at the door by willowy and patrician Dora Caesar. She was gracious and cordial. Her husband wasn't home yet, an absence that went on and on and on.

The first hour passed with reasonable speed, although it was obviously not to be the kind of party Joseph Moncure March wrote about. Only one other couple was present, Nat Dorfman and his wife, sedate newcomers on the Hollywood scene.

Nat had left his career as a publicity man on Broadway to try his luck as a Hollywood writer. He was happily optimistic that he would make it big, a subject that helped while away the early evening as we waited for our host. If this party was going to fly wildly, it was starting with a sober liftoff. Our hostess did not offer drinks or, for that matter, anything else.

The night began to take on the aspects of a horror film, with slow tension building toward the unknown. Even Dora Caesar, charming as she was, looked the typical female character one finds in that genre—tall, regal yet forbidding in a silk, all black, floor-length dress. She periodically implored us not to leave because Arthur would be terribly hurt.

It was after ten when he staggered in, drunk and pugnacious. The fact that Dorfman and I sat around for three hours was due to our innocence and timidity, grappling with an unfamiliar situation in a strange new surrounding. We paid for our stupidity.

Caesar lurched directly to his chair at the dinner table, his only excuse for his lateness was that he was unhappy with the bad news he was bringing but, as a friend, owed it to us to tell all. His revulsion with the report he was about to make was what made him linger at the bar of his country club.

With a writer's attention to details, he told us he had been on the polo field with three of the most important production executives in Hollywood: Joseph M. Schenck, Darryl Zanuck and Irving Thalberg. When told that Dorfman and I were his dinner guests, these Neros announced we were unacceptable citizens for Hollywood. Their collective thumbs turned down. We were marked for immediate destruction. "Beat it back to Broadway as fast as you can," advised Caesar. "You've been thrown to the lions. Don't try to fight it. You're through before you start . . ."

He was so convincing that our long-awaited meal went untouched; my wife had trouble holding back tears and the Dorfman complexions turned ashen.

I voiced some tentative doubt, not anxious to call our first Hollywood host a liar. My challenge to explain how our presence mattered to such busy men triggered a thunderous fusillade of words, punctuated with poundings that shook the table.

"Caesar knows! Caesar was there! Caesar has spoken!"

It didn't seem possible that Irving Thalberg, whose serious heart condition was well known to me, would be playing polo. But Caesar shook that off, claiming Thalberg's doctor had recommended this activity.

Finally we fled. I had an unhappy drive home, unable to convince my devastated wife that Caesar surely had been playing a practical joke. In the morning I could call her from the studio to report Thalberg didn't play polo ever, and was nowhere near Caesar's club the previous evening. Later that day she received a dozen American Beauty roses with an apologetic card. She tore up the card and sent it back with the roses.

If she couldn't take a joke, neither could the Dorfmans. They promptly returned to New York. But as he boarded the Santa Fe Railroad's crack train, Nat issued a friendly warning, meant for all Easterners in California: "Never buy anything you can't put on *The Chief!*"

Our second party, a comparative delight, was at a house in the Los Feliz section of Los Angeles shared by two bachelor Broadwayites, fellow transplants. Ben Thau was the newly appointed casting executive of MGM. He held that same position with Loew's Theatres in New York until plucked out of it by Louis B. Mayer, the head of the studio, who sent him west and then off to Europe with even fewer instruction than Thalberg gave me. Thau was a quiet, uncommunicative individual of whom it was said that when he opened his mouth, dust came out.

His cohost was Edgar Allen Woolf, an ebullient concoctor of vaudeville and revue skits during his Broadway incarnation. He had a huge shock of unruly red hair, a raucous laugh and a love of cooking. In a time when homosexuality was rarely exposed he made no secret of his leanings. "Benny and I have two things going for us in this house. He goes for the girls and I go for the boys!"

Woolf was one of four gagsters at MGM who were primarily script doctors. His job was to invent jokes and curtain lines that gave audiences a laugh before a scene dissolved or faded out. For him there was no deadline to deliver a screenplay. He took off every midweek to prepare his Saturday night parties. At this one, the guest of honor was a young platinum blonde. The reputation for wildness she gained in the years ahead wasn't apparent. Jean Harlow was quiet and reserved throughout the evening, staying demurely close to her mother, more buxom and almost as blonde.

After dinner, Woolf enlivened the party with his remembrance of a revue he wrote for New York's Madison Square Garden Roof. He had proudly invited his mother to attend its premiere, and his voice rose to a loud pitch as he described the events of that night.

"It was a disaster. I was booed. People were shouting, demanding their money back. Then, shots rang out. That mad playboy Harry K. Thaw, jealous because Stanford White had taken showgirl Evelyn Nesbit away from him, did it. He killed him right there, at ringside, the architect who designed and built the Garden."

The gunshots panicked Woolf's mother, already shaken by the violent reaction to her son's show. Over the tumult she could be heard screaming, "My God, they've shot my Edgar!"

Our third party was a glamorous and luxurious affair, given by one of the world's best-known humorists. With his wife and daughter by his side, tall, reserved and plump P. G. "Plummy" Wodehouse greeted us at the entrance to a huge peppermint-striped tent erected for the occasion on the back lawn of their rented Beverly Hills mansion. Here, indeed, was a cloud-level Hollywood party.

As soon as we arrived, Marie caught the eye of Rudolf Friml, composer of many popular operettas. Without a word to me, he took her by the hand and led her away. He held her hand through dinner and I suspect he would have held on, if he could, when called to the piano to play. However, with both hands busy, he just had her sit beside him. My glances through the evening revealed them in intense discussion, which went on until the party ended at two in the morning.

"What was that all about?" I asked on our way home.

"Oh," she said, airily, "he wants me to leave you and go to China with him."

Obviously, she had enjoyed that one much more than our previous parties.

"He certainly made it sound attractive," she said, sweetly. "A trip to the Orient with all expenses paid. He said that sort of thing goes on here all the time, but he was very complimentary about you. He said he admired your taste. So you see, you want to go to parties and be in the swim and now you are."

A few weeks later we attended a Friml operetta being revived in a cavernous auditorium in Los Angeles. The best seats I could get had us placed far back from the stage.

The composer made a grand entrance to an orchestral fanfare, smiling and bowing right and left as he sashayed down the aisle, arm in arm with two gorgeous Chinese girls in colorful silk kimonos.

"Have you ever wondered where you'd be now if you'd gone to China with him?" I asked.

She made a disdainful gesture at our remote seat location.

"I know exactly where I'd be. In the front row on the aisle!"

My three months were up. There was no time available for the writing I hoped to do, but Thalberg wanted me to go on running the story department, at a (slightly) higher salary.

Marie and I talked it over.

"If I quit now, people will think I wasn't any good and couldn't hold the job."

We agreed we didn't want that. Even a hint of failure in Hollywood could destroy a career for years. It was akin to that doomsday line that haunted every actor, director, writer and producer, "You're only as good as your last picture."

I remembered the fateful start of my own Hollywood career, arriving at precisely the moment the studio boss needed a story editor. The words he said that day came back to me. "If you'd shown up yesterday I'd have given you an assignment and forgotten about you."

My writing plans jettisoned, I was awash in a sea of writers.

Chapter Two

A new world opened up for writers when the movie *The Jazz Singer* premiered the night of October 6, 1927. In a few minutes, Al Jolson sang three songs, ad libbed a few lines of dialogue, and turned silent movies into a primitive form of cinema art.

Earlier experiments with sound had come and gone with no impact on how films were written. Until *The Jazz Singer*, scenario writers created the continuity of each proposed film, depicting the actions for the camera with little concern for what the actors said, as no one could hear them anyway. Title writers would take over when photography was complete and insert the rhetoric they thought audiences should be told.

They were addicted to simplistic, almost moronic description of visible scenes like "Came the Dawn," and they placed quotation marks around sentences to denote they were being said. The imagination of the watchers seemed to make those sentences audible.

When I arrived, two and a half years after the great change, the writing department payroll totalled fifty-five thousand dollars a week—an impressive figure for the time. Ten continuity and three title writers had survived. Twenty-seven were playwrights and novelists, recent additions, all far more literate than the authors they replaced, although a Hollywood newspaper columnist labeled them "Eastern scribblers" and angrily wondered why studios gave them shelter.

They were alien invaders, transients in a community where everyone from executives to back-lot workers were blood-brothers. The surviving scenarists did nothing to make life easier for the newcomers.

"We are the indispensable of the industry," said Carey Wilson, smugly. He was a graduate of the silent era but silence was anathema to him; he never used a single word when six would do. An associate said of him, "Ask him what time it is and he'll tell you how to make a watch."

The writers had become like designers in an automobile factory, but the difference was that when a car model was approved, it could roll off the production lines by the thousands, each one just like the one ahead and the one behind. Hollywood's movies, even when they followed a trend, had to contain new elements unlike those that had preceded them. Invention, imagination, and intelligence had to be applied to each one. To steer MGM to the Number One position and to keep it there, it wasn't necessary just to have writers, it was necessary to have the best.

The fifty-five thousand dollar payroll didn't bother Thalberg, whose mind was always on perfection. He had been skeptical of talkies when they first caught on, believing (and hoping) they would fade away, but finally accepted the inevitable and set out to make them to the best of his ability. He wanted superior writing and several times during my first days on the job reminded me to be alert to important literary talent and go after it at whatever cost. "Audiences will reach for quality but never stoop," he said one day. I thought it an impressive but dubious maxim.

Paul Bern, one of his supervisors, as producers were then called, dropped into my office to punctuate the importance of writers I might find. He was of short stature, soft-spoken, very well read, thoughtful, and extremely helpful to me as I stumbled along trying to catch on to the intricacies of my new job. "Never let your standards be less than great" was one of his early injunctions. It was indicative of the feelings the studio's five supervisors had as they followed Thalberg's leadership.

Money, and how to save it, was always in the mind of feisty General Manager Eddie Mannix, third from the top on the executive ladder of the studio, just below Mayer and Thalberg. Mannix looked like a bulldog and roared like a lion. He was known as Honest Eddie, a description he proudly propagated. He supervised the supervisors and, from that powerful position, notified me I was to preside over an economy meeting the upcoming Saturday morning. I was instructed to read the name of every writer on the payroll and discuss in depth their salaries, assignments, and progress. He expressed a fervent desire that I chop a number of them from their studio connections.

The day before these executions were to take place, one of Thalberg's secretaries called to say I was not to mention his sister Sylvia, who was a working writer. Louis B. Mayer's office called to say that the name of his niece wasn't to be brought up, and Supervisor Harry Rapf made a similar request about his son. All these youngsters were at work on assignments and while they would never win awards, were moderately competent. I toyed with an idea of ignoring the requests.

"Everyone knows they work here," I told the remarkable Mrs. Corbaley. "Who do they think they're fooling?"

She gave me a warm smile. "Don't be a wayward child." Obviously, if nepotism begins at home, the studio was it.

Saturday brought one of those great Southern California mornings when the mountains and beaches lived up to their advertised allure, and the men who gathered in Mannix's office were usually found at a golf course, a tennis court, or a beach club. They straggled in with understandable irritation. I was already aware of their literary leanings.

Paul Bern preferred women writers and sexy stories; genial Bernie Hyman made adventure-type films while rarely venturing outdoors himself; serious-minded Hunt Stromberg could never see the point of a joke but preferred sophisticated material for his productions; and Laurence Weingarten leaned entirely toward comedies. The fifth man was veteran Harry Rapf, whose diversified tastes ranged from comedy to stories with weepy, emotional themes.

They produced under Thalberg's direction, and like him,

without screen credits. Although anonymous to the public, they enjoyed recognition as an elite of picture-makers in Hollywood society. Neither Mayer nor Thalberg showed up that morning.

With the meeting in gear, I passed quickly over contractees whose dependability assured a need for them. Each supervisor controlled one or more. They would rather lose their wives or mistresses before giving up a favored writer. It brought my list down to thirty. Thalberg's favorites, Frances Marion, Anita Loos, Charlie MacArthur, Laurence Stallings and John Meehan, brought it down to twenty-five. They were untouchable.

I had no need to mention Wodehouse, whose contract for a year at two thousand dollars a week was about to expire. He had come to conquer movie writing but failed to get the hang of it. Too late, it was discovered that his droll dialogue made good reading but was otherwise unspeakable. No need to put his head on the chopping block, it was already there.

A quartet of high-powered gag writers were indeed as indispensible as Carey Wilson claimed. Al Boasberg, Edgar Allan Woolf, Ralph Spence and Bob "Hoppy" Hopkins were never at a loss for a sight gag or a curtain line. Secure in the knowledge their jokes were vital, they could heap contempt on their bosses and get away with it. They did it right to their faces.

Harry Rapf had a long, large nose. When Rapf was leaving for a sea voyage that summer, Hoppy advised him not to stick his head out of a porthole or "the boat will turn around!" As I sped past their names, not even Eddie Mannix's increasing scowl slowed me down.

The examination of the remaining names consumed the balance of that Saturday morning. The supervisors protected the writers under their command; to abandon them could mean killing the stories they were working on and that amounted to an admission of personal failure. Between their defense and my appeal for their continued employment, the session neared an end without a single writer being dismissed. Finally only one was left.

Walter Wise was a junior writer, hired more for his future than his presence. His salary was fifty dollars a week. He came last because the initial W placed him there alphabetically, since Wodehouse was disqualified and Woolf a perennial.

The grim jaw of Eddie Mannix was even grimmer while I argued not only that the youth's stipend was miniscule, but to throw him out at this time was to lose the value of the teaching he had received. Paul Bern and Bernie Hyman helped save Wise by offers to include him in story conferences.

A long morning over, I picked up my list and headed out the door and as I passed through it I heard Mannix grumble, "The trouble with our new story editor is that he *likes* writers!"

Chapter Three

E|very Monday morning brought a different type of get-together, one that revealed the importance the studio attached to acquiring story material. Thalberg and his supervisors suspended all other work to consider and decide which tales should be bought to keep the wheels of production rolling.

They assembled in the Spanish-style cream-colored villa with orange tile roof that served as the in-studio residence of the executives.

The same group that attended the failed Saturday shoot-out arrived at nine and seated themselves around a long dining table. The menu was food for thought as they digested plots from the week's cascade of submissions Kate Corbaley and I would present to them.

Corbaley was the star. She sat at the head of the table. Thalberg was a supporting player, down at the other end, a rapt listener.

Story telling is surely one of the world's oldest arts and many Scheherazades are noted through history, but there was a special finesse to Kate Corbaley. She never forgot a detail, never needed to retrace her steps, failings common to less talented yarn spinners.

She injected color, clarity, and characterizations that might well have won the envy of the original author. Because she literally thought in pictures, she could embroider a plot into a movie with elements its creator might have overlooked. Our listeners knew this. They were absorbed by the plot turns she offered them. Knowing we had made changes, they often asked our reasons for doing so. Corbaley had firm opinions on the worth of every story she presented. She was not above branding some as "trash," her favorite disparagement, but excused that classification on grounds that it provided elements some star's fans might want to see.

Thalberg possessed an extraordinary ability to visualize a complete feature film from a thumbnail sketch of a story or even a single thematic line. He recognized literary names and relished good titles. It wasn't unusual for him to project who would write the scenario, who would direct it and who would star in it, even before we entered into negotiations to buy the rights. Sometimes the rights weren't available after all, which led him to say regretfully, "A story never looks as good as when the other fellow buys it—or as bad as when we do." But his willingness to give stories top priority sped the decisions we needed and made my job infinitely easier.

And there was fun in the story meetings too, a quota of comedy that offset the seriousness of the business at hand. Following the telling of a supposed life of Mary Magdalen, Harry Rapf leaned forward and asked, "Can it be done in modern dress?"

"Not while I'm here," said Thalberg.

Rapf dismissed a book offered to him.

"Take out the essentials and what have you got?" he asked. Then, good-naturedly, he joined in the laughter.

Bernie Hyman, who had accepted a book Kate told, lamented that after reading the material, he found it far from what he had heard. Thalberg shrugged and said, "Shoot the story Kate told!"

The way this coterie of executives looked up to Thalberg was exemplified by their tender, loving concern for his fragile health. They tried to guard him against germs, constantly warned him against venturing out in bad weather without an overcoat or straining his heart with exhausting hours. When asked about this, Bernie Hyman replied with candor and a gift of prophecy, "As long as Irving lives we're all great men."

I shared their admiration for Thalberg, with whom I was now in daily association, able to observe his methods close up. I was also developing boundless admiration for Kate Corbaley.

Born on the steamer *Alaska* at sea off the coast of Mexico, she grew up in San Bernardino and recalled friendships with Indians driven down from the hills in winter. After graduating Stanford at Palo Alto, California, she became a librarian there.

Hunt Stromberg, filming a picture on location, had stopped by in search of a book he wanted. He was so taken by her knowledge of stories he induced her to come to work for him in Hollywood.

Stromberg was then associated with independent producer and pioneer film maker, Thomas H. Ince, for whom Corbaley acquired tremendous admiration and devotion.

She was stunned and skeptical when Ince mysteriously died aboard a yacht cruising off the coast of Southern California. His companions included the newspaper tycoon William Randolph Hearst, film stars Marion Davies and Charles Chaplin. Celebrity power in Southern California was enormous. Its influence reached into all corners of politics and law. Quite often, Kate spoke to me of the death of Ince and her remembrance of the man always brought tears to her eyes. The mystery of what happened to him was conjured up in her mind every time we discussed a tale of sudden death and dark deeds at sea; she believed a rumor he was shot, and never accepted the coroner's report that her former and beloved boss died of a heart attack. But the coroner's report was the official version.

With the dissolution of the Ince Studio, Stromberg moved to MGM and brought Corbaley with him. When she died, long after the gaudy spree of the Thirties, I was a pall-bearer. Louis B. Mayer and I sat side by side on a church bench. During the eulogy, he leaned close and said, "I would rather have lost any star than this woman."

Her faculty for knowing stories was, I thought, all the more remarkable because she never stepped beyond the borders of California. Yet she was as informed as any world-traveler about the theatre in New York, London and Paris; the stage hits and misses, the books that were selling best around the world. Although her mind was filled with their plots, she remembered every one, conjuring up their details at the mere hint of a title.

Several times I urged her to go to New York to see Broadway shows in full bloom, but she never did. She didn't need to. She preferred to read plays and think of them in movie terms; stage performances and directions would divert her. I suspected another reason, more closely allied to family. Single-handedly, she was raising four young daughters and didn't want to be a continent away from them, even for a short time. Her husband had run off; on the one occasion we discussed him, I could see her eyes go cold.

That marital disaster contributed to Kate's very personal relationship with scenarist Florence Ryerson. Florence's husband also deserted her, rather injudiciously leaving a note that he was taking off for the South Sea Islands with his new love. Some while later, he reappeared at his wife's door, a happy smile on his face, arms outstretched.

"Darling, I'm back," he exclaimed.

Ryerson slammed the door violently in his face, preferring a new love of her own.

Kate's constant retelling of this feminine triumph, so contrary to conventional yarns of suffering and subservient females, always sent her into gales of laughter. She was obviously primed to slam her door equally hard if Charles Corbaley ever came back.

There was never a doubt in my mind that Kate was strongly feminist; few of the males on the writing staff were her friends. Her attachments to her own sex among authors was oddly mixed, she hated some and loved others. Of them all, her deepest affection was reserved for Frances Marion, the most reliable scenario writer I ever knew, certainly the most inventive and the most generous.

Kate met Frances Marion when she first came down from San Francisco, eager to break into film writing but pragmatic enough to bring along a letter that recommended her as an experienced servant girl. It was Frances's first original story. She wrote it herself.

She was a resourceful creator of original stories. Few surpassed her abilities in that area. That talent alone gave her enormous value to Thalberg. In addition, she could turn them into practical screenplays tailored to his stars. *Min and Bill* and *Camille* are two of the more memorable examples of her extraordinary gifts.

Old-timers at the studio loved to talk to me about her, their reminiscences inevitably recalling how beautiful she was. "Ravishing" was the word used most often and there were plenty of photographs to prove it. Middle-aged when I met her, she was still radiantly attractive.

She dropped in on Kate periodically. Then the office door would be closed to the world so they might enjoy their "private gossip," as Kate described those sessions. Screams of laughter would issue through the locked portal.

Frances habitually bestowed presents on lesser workers involved with films she scripted, a wardrobe woman would receive jewelry, an assistant cameraman might be given a painting, a bit of sculpture, a valuable antique *objet d'art*. She bought cars for secretaries, handing over the keys with a simple, "I know you can use this." She gave collaborative screen credits to writers of her acquaintance, sometimes when they never touched pen to paper.

Lorna Moon, a young Scottish secretary who had been assigned to Frances, was felled by tuberculosis. Doctors said the dry climate of Arizona offered the only chance to prolong her life. Frances gave her the money she needed.

From Arizona, Lorna wrote of her wish to repay her benefactor. To do so, she had started to write a novel. Frances informed her the money was a gift, she did not intend it would be repaid. Then Lorna wrote that it was her dream that Frances would fashion her book into a great motion picture, one that would make them both proud.

Excited letters from the desert reported the progress of Lorna's book. "It's finished! A publisher has taken it!" Then,

"It's in print! The galleys are on their way to you." She wanted to bring them but her doctor forbade it; her strength was waning.

While waiting for it, Frances and Kate prepared Thalberg and the supervisors with praise for the book they had not seen. When it came, they pored through it, passing the pages from one to the other. Their spirits sank. *Dark Star* was a drab narrative of poverty and tragedy on the Scottish moors.

It had been scheduled to be told at the coming Monday morning meeting. The supervisors were eager to hear it, the advance build-up was impressed in their minds. Kate promised Frances she would do her best, aware that though she wielded influence on her listeners, it wouldn't be enough to sell Lorna's sad and tragic plot.

She gave her usual preliminary discourse, the background behind the story, reminded them that they knew the girl who was ill on the desert, spoke of the merits of purchasing a brand new novel before any rival producers saw it, tried to get them to desire a story she knew they wouldn't like very much when they heard it. She was like a conductor striving to create harmonies in an orchestra to offset the weakness of the composer's music. Finally, she took a deep breath and edged into the telling.

At that moment, Frances burst in. She asked Thalberg to let her describe the story, explaining that she knew it better than Kate because of her closeness to Lorna Moon and familiarity with her writing. She managed a quick look of apology at Kate but it wasn't necessary—Kate's face indicated her relief!

Frances launched into the earthy antics of two salty characters named Min and Bill, in and around a fishing pier at San Pedro, California. She brought the two roustabouts to life, picturing an absolute natural for costars Marie Dressler and Wallace Beery, the fun climaxed with a heart-tugging fade-out. The supervisors besieged Thalberg for the assignment to produce the film.

The prize went to Harry Rapf, who claimed, "It's right down my alley."

Frances kindly suggested to the busy man he not waste time reading the book, because, "I dropped out a few scenes having nothing to do with the movie." She would write the screenplay exactly as she told it.

On the screen, the credits of *Min and Bill* read, "From the book, *Dark Star,* by Lorna Moon." It was directed by Frances's husband, tall, gangling George Hill, a heavy drinker, a former cinematographer whose directing credits were mainly action melodramas. Frances sat on the set beside him throughout the production. She and Kate were ecstatic about the way they had put over their friend's wish; it was part of the fun, a joke on their bosses, adding flavor to their working routine as well as a triumph for their sex.

Not that women's rights were threatened. Their status on the studio's intellectual staff needed no enhancement. Women were on a par with men, their salaries in many cases higher than those of the males with whom they worked. Thalberg was attracted to stories that dealt with feminine problems. He sensed special value in them. "Wives and shop girls can always get their men to the movies they want to see, but a man can't get a woman to one that doesn't interest her," he said.

The whole world of moviegoers flocked to *Min and Bill* but Lorna Moon died before she could see the film she inspired. Nor did she hear Marie Dressler say, when she won the Academy Award for her part in it, "You can have the best producer and best director but it won't make any difference if you don't have the story!"

Chapter Four

$\boxed{W}$ill it make a movie?"
That question was in my mind whenever I heard a short anecdote or read about a honeymoon, a divorce, or a murder. It could be a plot born in a Hollywood writer's imagination or a classic tale in some ancient tome, but whatever its source, "Yes" was the only answer. "Anything a camera can focus on can make a movie," I observed, but Kate Corbaley wasn't impressed. "Okay," she said. "But is there an audience for it?"

At a Monday morning meeting Thalberg reflected along those same lines. "I can make a movie out of *Mrs. Rorer's Cookbook!* But I'm not sure anyone will go see it."

On the alert to every story possibility that might satisfy the studio's appetite, Corbaley marched into my office with the theatrical section of *The New York Times.*

Under a Berlin dateline, a small item stated that German entrepreneur Max Reinhardt had produced *Menschen im Hotel* in Berlin. It dealt with a few guests in a large urban hotel during thirty-six hours. It had closed after five performances.

"This reads like a movie," said Kate.

"What do I do now?" I asked, repeating what I had asked her a dozen times those first weeks on the job.

"Tell the New York office to rush you a copy of the play."

Someone had decreed during MGM's emerging years that anything east of the Mississippi must clear through the New York office. Lengthy night letters carried the studio's needs across that border, its requests channeled through the Western

Union operator who had a broom-closet-sized space inside the building that housed the executive offices.

I telegraphed my desire for *Menschen im Hotel* to Bertram Bloch, whom I had known in New York.

Bloch was one of two editors in the Eastern story department, and he concentrated on playscripts only. I learned it the hard way, because I wired him during my first week at the studio to send me galleys of a new Zane Grey western novel. He didn't. Instead, he wired back a message tinged with faint reproach informing me that requests for books must always be addressed to the other editor, Nina Lewton, because she handled books. Thereupon I redirected my request for Zane Grey's book some twenty-five hundred miles and never made the mistake again. Mrs. Lewton's office was a few steps from his own, about the same distance as Kate Corbaley's from mine.

The playscript arrived promptly. Its swift delivery gave an obvious indication someone in New York wanted to make a movie sale.

That someone was Harry Moses, an American underwear manufacturer from New York. He had seen the play at the Theatre Am Nollendorfplatz in Grundgens. Among its patronizing reviews was one suggesting *Menschen im Hotel* might survive importation, so Moses, with no theatrical experience, bought all rights, including film, for five thousand dollars. It was his silver anniversary present for his wife Elsa, who aspired to a footlight debut in the role of the prima ballerina. She planned to make her entrance carrying her own pet Pekinese, exactly as author Vicki Baum had written in her stage direction.

Before turning to writing, Vicki Baum had danced ballet, then changed course and became a harpist. She studied at the Vienna Conzertverein, and played the harp professionally at Darmstadt, the only woman among ninety men. She also gave lessons in harp to support herself while writing novels.

Menschen im Hotel was her tenth published book. She described its characters as the most hackneyed she could find, involved in ordinary situations. To make readers sorry for them she added hidden tragic dimensions that delved into the meanings of their lives during the hours they stayed in the hotel.

At the urging of play agent Edmund Pauker, she permitted a friend of his to try his hand at adapting the book for the Berlin stage. He did a dismal job, whereupon she retrieved it and wrote the version that Bloch sent me to read. That presented an unexpected problem; it was in German.

Foreign language translators were available, working for the studio when called on. However, *Menschen im Hotel* didn't seem to require any urgency, so the playscript was lying on my desk and no translator had been summoned when a very charming Hungarian director showed up.

Paul Fejos had just signed an MGM contract. Thalberg told him to see what material was on hand that might interest him for his first film at the studio. When he said he could read German, I told him what I knew of Vicki Baum's play and asked him to report if he found any merit in it.

He was waiting, wild with enthusiasm, when I came in the next morning. I took him to Thalberg, where Fejos described what he read and begged for a chance to direct it. Thalberg agreed, with reservations. While the wheels of the story department would now roll toward a film version, he would assign Fejos to a program picture to test the director's talent.

The German play had flopped so badly, opening and closing almost simultaneously, it seemed unlikely that much negotiation would be needed to buy the film rights. Also, we surmised (and this proved to be true) no other film company paid any attention to the clipping that stimulated Corbaley's interest, so acquiring it would be clear sailing. It was given a low priority as we followed our regular daily routines.

I took the script back from Fejos and asked Paul Bern, the studio's most urbane and erudite supervisor, for his opinion. His teutonic background was strongly impressed on me, and he expressed pleasure at the opportunity to read a new German play. That pleasure increased when he felt there was the making of an extraordinary film in it. He asked Thalberg that it be assigned to him, whereupon I informed Bloch we didn't want to lose it.

The business arrangement was simple. The studio was interested in the film; Producer Moses in the stage. Advisors had already told him they estimated twenty-six thousand dollars would be enough to open on Broadway. He agreed that, for an investment of half that amount, he would give MGM the film rights. He also agreed to repay the studio's thirteen thousand dollars out of the very first box-office returns.

At worst, then, we were buying the movie rights to a story we wanted for thirteen thousand dollars; at best, we might get a refund. No one in New York or Hollywood expected to get it for free but that was exactly what happened, turning the sale into the greatest movie purchase of all time.

However, without the power to foresee the future, even in this land of make-believe, the studio sought to protect its investment. We sent the script to a freelance Hollywood translator, William A. Drake, after learning that Moses had not yet done so in New York. Such negligence raised doubts about his competence to put the play on Broadway, so we began issuing suggestions. The first was that he ally himself with a seasoned producer.

A functioning Broadway producer was Herman Shumlin, who used a reader, with whom he was romantically involved, to comment on playscripts submitted to him. She, too, liked *Menschen im Hotel.* The reader was Lillian Hellman, whose writing career was on hold but who would ultimately outrank all the males swarming around her, vastly outdistancing them and her husband, Arthur Kober, who was also an aspiring writer.

Moses went to see Shumlin's current Broadway show, *The Last Mile,* and recruited him to join his company. There was no budgetary allowance for an experienced dramatist, so William A. Drake's English translation of Vicki Baum's German was used when the play went into rehearsal.

To maintain our hopes that the show would have a professional look to it, we also suggested a careful assessment of

Mrs. Moses and her Pekinese, as their appearance in the cast seemed suspiciously amateur and the role of the ballet dancer was an extremely important one. After her first rehearsal, Mrs. Moses concurred and withdrew.

And then the miracle that is ever present in the worlds of film and theatre occurred. There was incredible, fantastic magic onstage at the National Theatre the evening of November 13, 1930. With virtually the same elements that didn't jell in Berlin, the play, now called *Grand Hotel,* became the hit of the year in New York.

Vicki Baum, vacationing in Russia, received a cable from a former harp pupil, the wife of orchestra leader Eugene Ormandy: GRAND HOTEL GREATEST BROADWAY SUCCESS IN THIRTY YEARS, CONGRATULATIONS. She thought someone was playing a joke.

There was credit for everybody and Herman Shumlin and Lillian Hellman claimed a major part in the New York newspapers. Shumlin mourned his failure to have the movie rights which he publicly valued at more than a hundred thousand dollars. What seemed tragedy to him seemed comedy to us as, in our view, a good portion of the show's success was due to the demands of the studio. Shumlin and Moses were agonized by the sight of thirteen thousand dollars shoveled into the box office within hours after opening night. All of them would go to the film company, and Shumlin acted as if his pockets had been picked.

The momentum of that Broadway hit catapulted Vicki Baum's book version onto best-seller lists around the country and won her a studio contract and a ticket to the Writer's Building. *Menshen im Hotel* eclipsed all her other achievements, causing her to later mourn, "I spent twenty-five years thinking about it, six weeks to write it and the rest of my life trying to live it down."

When, as a boy, I first discovered the joy of reading, two American novels were my favorite books. Good stories about attractive people whose lives seemed attractive to me, the two books were F. Scott Fitzgerald's *This Side of Paradise* and Cyril Hume's *Wife of the Centaur.*

Scott Fitzgerald was, of course, a literary celebrity, later famed for his high standing among the drinking classes.

Cyril Hume had no special fame, although another book, *The Golden Dancer,* had captured accolades from the critics. He was a virtually unknown author whom I admired from afar.

When I came to MGM, I discovered it wasn't so afar after all. In fact, he was parked just a few doors from me, in the writer's building, waiting out the final weeks of a three-month contract. He had failed at a couple of early assignments and the supervisors gave up on him as a screen writer. He survived the Saturday morning economy meeting because of the obligation of his contract but when it expired, he would be gone. He knew it, the studio executives knew it and I was told about it in detail by Eddie Mannix, so I knew it, too. In fact, Mannix, in his blunt way, said I was only going to waste my time if I found him an assignment, and the sooner the studio was rid of him, the better.

Under those circumstances, I made no effort to introduce myself to Hume, even if I could admit to being a fan. It would only spotlight my own ineffectiveness as an executive, like dropping in on someone sentenced to death and thanking him for past favors, a true study in frustration.

At that time I became involved in seeking some sort of play doctor to administer to a very sick film. *Trader Horn* was to be the type of adventure film that audiences customarily loved, with animals and explorers, thrills and romance, all neatly packed into one exotic package. It was shot in Africa under the supervision of Bernie Hyman. It wasn't exactly shot—a better description would be "half-shot," and that could be taken literally and cynically.

The actors and crew, under the direction of W. S. Van Dyke, had gone to Africa soon after sound invaded the industry. Early uncertainty whether that dimension would become permanent in movies probably contributed to the sprawling jigsaw of incomplete sequences they brought back to California.

Nobody had been able to figure out what to do with this blurred compilation of celluloid. A scenic attraction for studio-visiting tourists was a pair of seven-foot African chiefs who, having been established in the film as important characters, were loaned to the company by the British Governor who ruled Kenya, their native land. These majesties were living in two large tents on the back lot, waiting to finish their roles in the stalled movie. They refused to accept quarters in a Culver City hotel because it meant descending to the level of the other guests, whom they saw as white commoners. Their every demand was being met while they were being maintained in considerable luxury at the expense of *Trader Horn*'s budget. Their demands included female companionship, supplied with the help of the studio's shoeshine boy who recruited them from Los Angeles' black community on Central Avenue. The Africans agreeably disregarded the lack of tribal understanding of these ladies.

The continued upkeep of two royal Africans was only a small part of the movie's problems. Bernie Hyman implored me to help him find a writer who would salvage the dormant production.

I entertained the strong belief at that time, that a writer did his best work on subjects he generally knew about, so I concentrated my search on those who wrote tropical dramas. John Colton, on the studio staff, had dramatized Somerset Maugham's *Rain* and also wrote a steamy and bizarre melodrama, *The Shanghai Gesture*. But he failed miserably when assigned to *Trader Horn*.

My next suggestion was Leon Gordon, whose *White Cargo*—a sizzling drama of passion and decadence in the tropics—was a Broadway hit. When I located him, he was in Australia and his reply to my cabled offer said he was flattered and would look me up the next time he was in California, but right now he was busy getting married.

Thalberg didn't agree with my theory that the writer had to feel a relationship to the material he worked on. He said, "It's good discipline for writers to work on stories that are foreign to them."

I didn't agree with him and told him so, but decided to widen the scope of my search. I was also motivated by pure desperation, because Hyman was beginning to look at me as though my delay in finding the right screen writer was contributing to his predicament with the film. Therefore, I told him of my boyhood admiration for Cyril Hume's book. With what was evidently similar desperation, Hyman agreed to meet with him.

Hume was actually in the process of packing up his belongings when I walked into his office and told him why I was there. As we headed for Hyman's office, he mentioned that he knew of the *Trader Horn* mess (it was hardly a secret), and he had even taken it upon himself to read the book. But he made no effort to help. He felt that having sat for weeks without as much as a phone call, such volunteering would seem presumptuous. It was apparent that this serious-minded, white-haired author also had an un-Hollywood streak of shyness.

I sat beside him a few moments in Hyman's office and left when the supervisor began explaining he would screen a sequence he felt contained the most important elements of the main theme. How Hume would write it would serve, in effect, to test his grasp of the story.

Late that afternoon I returned and walked in on an extraordinary sight: both men weeping. Hyman thought Hume's scene exceeded his greatest expectations of how it should go, while Hume reacted to Hyman's exultant reaction so emotionally that both men had burst into tears.

That was a turning point in the life of Cyril Hume. His revised screenplay fused the disconnected sequences of *Trader Horn* into such a success the film went out as a roadshow attraction at raised admission prices.

Its success after its close brush with disaster prompted the team of Hyman, Hume and Van Dyke to take on *Tarzan, The Ape Man,* which, although fiction, was a kind of literary cousin to the alleged factual life of *Trader Horn.*

The concept of an English boy raised by jungle gorillas was born in the brain of Edgar Rice Burroughs, who operated a veritable Tarzan factory a few miles north of the studio in the San Fernando Valley. Ghostwriters were manufacturing books and newspaper comics depicting these popular adventures in a town appropriately named Tarzana.

Thalberg had enthusiastically approved the filming of *Tarzan* before leaving for a vacation and told me he considered it valuable to the point that, if I had to, I could pay a hundred thousand dollars for the rights.

So I entered into negotiations with Burroughs, who came to my office with an aide in charge of his business affairs. We quickly agreed that the time was ripe for a topgrade film feature; there had been a couple of low-budget Tarzans in the past, films that Burroughs dismissed as lacking the quality he hoped for. In this amiable climate he suggested a hundred thousand would be a fair price and I countered with an offer of fifteen thousand.

They walked out and a few days later I upped our offer to twenty-five. He came down to seventy-five. In this seesaw manner we finally arrived at forty thousand. When the deal was concluded, Burroughs' aide said, gloatingly, "We were so anxious to have MGM make this picture that if you had held out long enough you would have got it for nothing."

Stung, I snapped back, "If you had held out long enough you would have got your hundred thousand."

Cyril Hume's ability with exotic screen adventures was closer to Thalberg's theory than mine. Hume was so good at depicting jungle life he was first choice thereafter on a whole string of movies the studio would make along that line.

Assigning Hume to *Trader Horn* was a coup for me and I had reason to be proud of it. But there was an ironic side, one that robbed it of any sense of triumph. I had suggested him because I thought so highly of a book he wrote years before, and I would have dearly loved to read more from him. But his successes with *Trader Horn* and *Tarzan* tied his life to screen writing forever. He never wrote another book.

Chapter Five

Alady agent who found jobs for young actors and actresses dropped in on me one morning and asked, "Can you give me twenty minutes and show me how to write my book?"

I resisted the temptation to say, "It may take twenty-five," because she might not recognize the sarcasm and I'd be stuck with her. Instead, I suggested she find her own way as any guidelines from me might badly affect her own natural style. I even said I'd read her book as soon as it was finished. She accepted this as a very kindly offer, which it wasn't. I was reasonably sure (as was indeed the case) her book would never be born. Few who wrote books asked how to do it.

She set me to thinking about the many sudden strangers around me driven by a compulsion to write. It was all due, of course, to my position with such a prestigious studio. Everyone I met had a story or an idea they wanted me to know about. It was as playwright George S. Kaufman said: "Ask anybody how's your second act coming and they'll tell you."

Writing was a curious and perilous career. Even the professionals on the studio staff all started as amateurs when they opted for the precarious life of a writer, ignoring the depressing tales of loneliness and desperation, sadness and starvation that were its legendary hazards down through the ages.

Quite possibly, I thought, they were drawn to it by the well-publicized tales of authors who found inspirations in far-flung outposts, among them the indomitable Rudyard Kipling in India, Evelyn Waugh in Africa, Somerset Maugham in the

Orient, Noel Coward aboard an oil tanker. Who wouldn't want to create undying literature—well, reasonably undying—in such exotic climates? Then, too, there was *La Boheme's* free love and camaraderie at the Cafe Momus, or the intellectual stimulation enjoyed at the Mermaid Tavern, Le Deux Magot or the Algonquin Round Table. Who wouldn't want to be in on such festivities?

It may be questionable whether such lofty concepts went on in Hollywood, but there were many such assemblages. Each of the major studios had writers buildings, all filled with conviviality and high spirits. In them one wrote and mixed with one's contemporaries, working on stories for movies amid a cacaphony of laughter and arguments, the shuffling of chairs, footsteps of restless pacers, flasks slapped on desks and the click of occasional typewriters.

There was the click of dice, too. At Paramount, Zoe Akins, a formidable playwright, knocked on the office door of her neighbor, Joseph Mankiewicz.

"I do believe I hear Mace," she said, in her clipped British accent.

"Not mace," replied Joe. "Dace."

A sight that attracted all eyes at the studio was imperious Cecil B. DeMille, striding about in a white safari outfit with black boots, flanked by a fawning entourage of all sexes.

He was at MGM on loan-out from his home studio, Paramount, directing the second of two big-budget spectacles. It was hoped his films would make big bucks, as many had in the past, a period that fan magazines and film historians referred to as the Cecil B. DeMillenium.

However, *Madam Satan* was destined to be as spectacular a failure as its predecessor, *Dynamite,* which was already down the drain of theatres everywhere. By mutual agreement, Thalberg distanced himself from the famous director during the making of these productions. I had no contact with him, either, because he created the stories and brought along his own writing staff.

I never got to know three of the four scenarists he brought—Jeanie MacPherson, Gladys Unger and Elsie Janis. The fourth other lady on his staff I did want to meet, having heard much about her, her love affairs and sexy wisecracks. Her sarcastic comments as book and drama critic and her stinging one-liners seemed to far outnumber the poems and short stories that comprised her literary output. I was already in awe of Dorothy Parker when two similarly transplanted wits from New York, Robert Benchley and Donald Ogden Stewart, marched her into my office to introduce her.

The legendary sexpot of New York's literati was nearing her fortieth birthday, a petite albeit plump brunette, not as cute as I had pictured her but bright and charming. We hit it off well and I received permission from Thalberg to delay her return to Paramount while I sought an assigment for her.

However, he grumbled about her being trouble, saying, "She thinks it's smart to bite the hand that feeds her."

He recited some of the stories circulating through Hollywood about her, that when DeMille brought her to MGM and she was asked her preference for an office, she said, "All I need is room to lay my hat and a few friends." He also claimed she pried a plate from a door near her office, and used it to cover her name. It read "MEN."

But her attitude was what he feared most. Ridicule of the industry was a sore point with him. He reacted sharply against all who indulged in it, and while he might engage in jokes and repartee of that nature with his staff, it was not for public consumption.

He felt victimized one time when he attempted a show of humor and sent a memorandum to the Music Department, newly operative then with the coming of sound. "As MGM is a major studio, please instruct our composers not to use minor chords." The memo was taken seriously and posted in the department until Thalberg rushed over and removed it.

His uneasy feelings about Dorothy Parker had an effect on the studio supervisors. They reported she called all studio executives "cretins" and leaned out of her office window shouting, "Get me out of here, I'm as sane as any of you!"

On hearing this, Thalberg said, "Oblige her." I did as I was told, but she and I remained friends the rest of her life. Her main contribution during her MGM period was a plaintive song lyric, "How Am I To Know?"

All the variables that turn human beings into writers were visible in the studio. It was believed that dramatists and novelists dealt best with made-up plots. Biographers knew real-life situations. Journalists also had great value because they were accustomed to writing under pressure. Producers clamored for them, believing their training to meet deadlines would help them.

But the flow of incoming authors also brought disappointments as the studios often gambled on men and women inexperienced at movie writing. They had their own habits of creation and many found it impossible to conform to the ways scenarios were created in conference.

I was responsible for recommending some of these writers. They tried and knew they failed.

Playwrights George Kelly and John Balderston and novelist James M. Cain fled, but not before handing back the money paid them. Oddly, I thought, the studio cared little for such gestures. I assume figuring how to account for these refunds made extra work for the bookkeeping department. Where in the records does one report "money returned by worker who didn't want it?"

Departure was far from the minds of the career scenarists. To them, Hollywood was home and movie writing a full-time occupation. Many were corrupted by the weekly paycheck and the imagined horror of being available without salary brought panic. I had calls from writers unable to curb their desperation, some openly confessing they couldn't think unless they were on a payroll.

Secure authors also had a tendency to gripe. Many were in the high-priced category with set salary standards and would rather endure weeks without work than accept fewer dollars than they were accustomed to receiving.

Within this creative circus, I was expected to select writers for their talents and not their attitudes. The choice of whom to put on what assignments was the target, not their opinions of the working arena. Some took the high road and some took the low while I, perforce, stayed in the middle.

Around me sounded the loud cries of the Dissatisfieds, occasionally dimmed by the pleasant quiet of the Satisfieds. Almost all bemoaned the inability to write as they pleased, but the price the studio paid them for their loss of liberty was acknowledged.

Playwright S. N. Behrman sized up the system with a remark that became a part of Hollywood history.

"It's slave labor and what do you get for it? A lousy fortune!"

Chapter Six

"I mitation," said Paul Bern, "is the sincerest form of box office." He enjoyed putting a new twist to old aphorisms and, in this case, he wanted to send me a message.

It was strange for Bern, the sophisticate, to favor the practice of imitation.

I accused him of being a phony intellectual when he knew novelty was entertainment's most desirable ingredient. "I can't believe the masses who go to the movies can stomach the same food at every meal," I told him loftily.

"Then find out for yourself," he said, and added as he walked away, "You will, my dear fellow!"

In that 1930–31 movie season, all the studios were making movies dealing with show business. The cycle began with *Broadway Melody* in 1928. A parade of films followed, about singers, dancers and actors desperate to attain the blessings of stardom. Naturally, they worked to a happy ending. Currently MGM had two variations on that theme, cabaret performers in *Night Hostess* and vaudeville folk in *Excess Baggage*. Both of them were doing creditable business while stretching credulity out of joint. Accuracy to life backstage took a severe beating at the movies.

On the screen, it mattered little whether art mirrored life or vice versa. In *42nd Street,* the film that Warner Brothers contributed to this cycle, an unrehearsed chorus girl was called on to step into the leading role of a big Broadway show.

"You're going out there a nobody," she was told, "and coming back a star."

The movie showed her do both and it did, indeed, do it for Ruby Keeler, who had formerly danced beside my wife Marie in a nightclub on Broadway. The musical hit of its time, *42nd Street* was a cinematic work of art, and it made Ruby Keeler a star.

But life—as I saw it—did not mirror art.

Our friend Jack Conway was directing *The New Moon,* an operetta-type film with Grace Moore and Lawrence Tibbett. Conway thought Marie had star quality. He wanted to do something about it and proposed that she appear in a shipboard scene in that film. I was all for it. The prospect of having my beautiful wife go out there a nobody and come back with a contract for thousands of dollars a week struck me as extremely attractive.

Director Conway planned to put Marie prominently near the camera for a photographic test. Then, in the course of the sequence, he would assign her some acting business that would show her off to audiences and hopefully make them want to see her again. The whole idea seemed the sort of opportunity devoutly desired by numberless young women around the world.

But Marie was highly unenthusiastic. At dawn on the day she was to make her film debut she took off grumpily for the studio. She returned in the evening still wearing traces of the make-up that had been daubed on her and indifferent to the point of not wanting to discuss it.

She was still asleep at six o'clock the next morning when the phone rang. A harassed assistant director barked, "Where the hell are you?" She told him she'd decided not to be a movie star and hung up.

She stared at me defiantly and said, "Why should I be over there at this ungodly hour, squeezed into an old Gypsy outfit, sitting around with nothing to do, my face smeared with goo, when I'm very happy and busy right here being your wife. If you wanted an actress instead of me you should have married

Helen Hayes like Charlie MacArthur did." Then she turned over and went contentedly back to sleep.

I took the next phone call, from Director Conway himself, and broke the news that here was one nobody who didn't give a damn about being a star. Let the show go on, I told him, but she wouldn't.

Marie's mention of Helen Hayes was no accident. That dedicated actress and her writer husband had become our close friends.

If I were asked my own favorite among screen writers, I would answer unhesitatingly Charlie MacArthur. Although his writings made splendid reading, whether in a book, play or movie, it was his personality that endeared him not only to me, but to everyone who came in contact with him. His fascinatingly irrational ways radiated like sunbeams. Alexander Woollcott, the corpulent "Town Crier" of magazine and radio fame, wrote, "At mention of his name everybody who knows him lights up and starts talking about him as if a marvelous circus had passed their way."

We met on a tennis court in Beverly Hills. I was schooled in the Manhattan practice of nursing three darkening balls through an entire summer. At our first meeting, Charlie brought a box of twenty-four new balls which he flung high in the air. When it hit the ground, it broke open and eight years' supply bounced around with what struck me as a symbol of Hollywood extravagance. We used them all and left them lying on the court three sets later.

An MGM contractee, MacArthur was then on loan-out to Samuel Goldwyn for a film he and long-time collaborator Ben Hecht pitched to that producer. They called the story *The Unholy Garden,* and for the plot they pictured some faraway oasis populated only by criminals on the lam.

This notion of a bizarre and lawless sanctuary was all they had when they went to Goldwyn's office and told him about it. Inventive to an enormous degree, Charlie and Ben managed to move the plot along by prearranged signals. During the telling, Hecht waved a cigar, MacArthur a cigarette. Placing it in the mouth indicated the speaker was out of inspiration, whereupon the other jumped in and took his turn. Fortunately for both, a secretary sat in on this weird meeting, for both admitted later that they had no recollection of what they were saying. But Goldwyn bought it then and there, and was mapping out his production for star Ronald Colman while the authors wrestled with the screenplay.

They worked on it during our tennis game, lobbing dialogue across the net.

"Chivalry," said Ben, "is the art of lying magnificently." He looked hopefully at his coauthor and was rewarded.

"After Colman says that, he bows and says, 'Madam, you never looked more beautiful.' "

Ben curtsied approvingly to his collaborator, missing a serve that Charlie smashed at him.

MacArthur's adoring wife had been on the stage almost as long as she could remember, having first appeared when she was six years old. Twenty-four years later, Helen Hayes was ready to make her film debut. Because Charlie was involved with numerous writing activities, all of them precariously incomplete, the scenario for his wife's movie was assigned to Frances Marion and Leonard Praskins.

Charlie teetered nervously between a desire to write this all-important media change for Helen and a fear that if it failed, the result would be fatal to her career. We went to Thalberg together to discuss his problem. The studio boss suggested Charlie keep his hands off until the film script was finished, then if he felt the need, he could do some rewriting.

Helen's movie wasn't scheduled to start until May 1931, still six months away, but Charlie had much to do so the MacArthurs settled into a splendid two-level, balcony-lined hacienda high on a hill behind the studio. Its driveway snaked through an avocado grove. Bedrooms were plentiful for Helen, Charlie, their infant daughter Mary, and houseguests already arrived or expected. From a balcony, downhill past the swimming pool, one could view the Los Angeles Basin, the nearby

Pacific and the snow-topped crest of Mount Baldy sixty miles away.

The owner of the hacienda lived in a small hut on the edge of the property, having sunk his fortune into raising avocados before learning the trees had to be seven years old before they bore fruit. He skulked around with nothing to do for the next five years but wait for the plants to grow up, scowling unpleasantly at the stream of friends thronging in daily to see Helen and her convivial husband.

Life at the hacienda was like a stage spectacle on which the curtain never descended. A collection of steamer trunks stood in the exact center of the living room. They belonged to Harold Ross, editor of *The New Yorker* magazine, who had sent them in advance of an intended visit. However, some unexplained complication snarled his travel plans. Through the winter the trunks remained in place like megalithic Stonehenge slabs. In the spring, Ross sent word he wouldn't be coming and wanted his trunks returned.

As an intermission between doings at the hacienda, Marie and I took off for a weekend with Charlie and Helen, driving south into Mexico, to the popular luxury spa at Agua Caliente.

In stark contrast to the expensive splendor of Caliente was its rundown neighbor, the border town of Tia Juana, whose delights ranged from an allegedly crooked jai alai fronton to brothels and streets full of bars where Americans could drown their thirst waiting for prohibition to be repealed.

A race track operated within walking distance to Caliente's Hotel and Casino. Like Chinese philosophers who relaxed their concentration on one problem by concentrating on another, movie folk found the frenzied life of Mexico's border ideal for escaping the frenzied life of Hollywood.

During the two-hour drive, Charlie recounted an episode wherein he and Ben Hecht were waiting in the library of Otto H. Kahn, millionaire godfather to starving artists. Charlie and Ben whiled away their time autographing a collection of bound volumes: "To Otto, without whose help these lines couldn't have been written, William Shakespeare" or "I drink to Otto, with gratitude for his outpouring assistance—Cicero." They also inscribed love to Otto from Plato and Oscar Wilde. If it really happened, they ruined a lot of rare editions.

Another of his stories had to do with Charlie dropping into the Manhattan apartment of blonde, leggy Peggy Hopkins Joyce, a much-married celebrity. The lady was out but her maid admitted him and left him alone. He found a closet full of powdered Jello and amused himself by dumping all of it into a bathtub of hot water, where it congealed and formed a rainbow-hued dessert, enough for a month of dinner parties. Thereupon he departed, unable to report on the lady's reaction when she discovered this questionable gourmet concoction. Marie told me later that you can't make Jello that way.

Peggy Hopkins Joyce was best known for marrying and divorcing wealthy men. She also made an occasional stage appearance that spotlighted her lack of acting talent. But her sex appeal was an acknowledged fact in New York's social and journalistic circles.

Charlie never explained his reason for dropping in on her. Helen admired him so it was clear she relished every memory he dredged up, even the many having to do with women. That many of them adored her husband was undeniable, his associations were widely known and publicized. It was reasonable to believe his adoring wife was certain he was more the hunted than the hunter.

Driving through the main street of Tia Juana she reminded him how he had told her of an earlier Christmas visit when he accompanied a friend to the town's largest whorehouse. Declining to participate in the usual services, he sat in the lobby and dispersed five dollar bills as holiday largesse to the girls. His innocent intention was misinterpreted, he told her, because their pride was hurt. They chased him out of the place, hurling imprecations and the money after him.

Besides grappling with *The Unholy Garden,* which wasn't developing with the ease with which they invented it for Goldwyn, Charlie and Ben had another problem. They sold the idea of a play, *Twentieth Century,* to producer Jed Harris before they wrote it. He was in New York with two acts and absolutely no word when or how it was to be completed. What he didn't know was that the authors didn't know either. A dark, sullen fellow obsessed with success, Harris was sending them threatening messages.

Nightly parties at MacArthur's hacienda took on an aura of spectacular grandeur. One evening, bare-handed fisticuffs between friends was scheduled as the feature event. The brothers Selznick squared off in a battle that Hecht announced would be fought to the death. He stood by the mantelpiece in the large front room, describing the nuances of the fight as if he was a radio sports announcer and goading them on to greater mayhem.

Stimulated further by snorts of liquor, David and Myron Selznick became progressively more ferocious. All the odds favored Myron, bulkier and far more muscular than his younger, pink-cheeked sibling. With no bell to measure the rounds, both gladiators grew bruised and bloodied. Finally, Myron bent low near the floor, his clenched fist describing a roundhouse arc. But instead of Myron's hand smashing David's cheekbone, David's cheekbone smashed Myron's hand. He retreated to a corner moaning in pain, while agent Leland Hayward presented the victor with a magnum of champagne amid cheers that could be heard down in the avocado grove.

Quite possibly, producer Jed Harris heard them. His patience on a short fuse, ignited by the indifference shown his demands that the authors complete *Twentieth Century,* he showed up at the hacienda screaming invectives. He refused to believe Charlie and Ben's perfectly logical explanation that they hadn't figured out the last act. He was physically escorted beyond the avocado grove but sneaked back repeatedly, jumping out from behind trees to waylay the authors, who continued to deny him access to the house.

All of this went on as Ben and Charlie sweated out the scenario of *Unholy Garden* under the impatient eyes of Samuel Goldwyn.

Meanwhile, Frances Marion and Leonard Praskins struggled with *Lullaby* for Helen. It was a soggy, sobby saga of mother-love in France around the time of World War I. Frances Marion and Leonard Praskins were trying hard to breathe some semblance of life into its conventional characters and dated plot line, but it was hard going. As 1931 drew to a close, they felt fortunate they still had five months to work on it.

When the studio acquired the film rights to *Grand Hotel,* little attention was paid to a clause in the contract that the movie couldn't be released until fifteen months after the November 1930 premiere of the stage version unless the show closed in the meantime. It seemed ludicrous to believe a play that lasted less than a week in Berlin would still be drawing packed houses in New York a year later. But *Grand Hotel,* having confounded these beliefs, was still going strong and the film couldn't be shown until March 1932.

In the fall of 1930, Thalberg and supervisor Bern began assembling a guest list for what was to be the studio's most important film of its time, with actual photography to start December 31. Author Vicki Baum was already on hand. She was preparing the scenario but had little to do but add a few touches to the Drake playscript, the translation that served so well on Broadway. A truly all-star cast, selected from MGM's great thespians, was being invited to fill the film's diverse roles.

An immense amount of soul-searching went on in meetings between Thalberg and Bern over the actor to portray the dissolute gambler, Baron Gaigern. John Gilbert, struggling with a career that plummeted with the coming of talkies, told his friends at the studio he was born for it, that many nights of drinking and carousing had been done in the company of Thalberg and Bern and they knew he could act the part without rehearsals. They knew, too, that he was desperate to win back his great lost love, Greta Garbo, who had an unrivaled lock on the role of the ballerina. In this film they could be lovers again as they were in their first movie, *Flesh and the Devil.* Here was history waiting to repeat itself.

But Gilbert lost the role to John Barrymore, who not only

could match him drink for drink and carousal for carousal, but also had a greater range of histrionics from his long stage career.

Losing the decision embittered Gilbert. It seemed to him to verify Eddie Mannix's summation of Thalberg: "He's a sweet guy but he can piss ice water!" For the rest of his life Gilbert maintained he would have been better in the part, but Thalberg countered with, "I make them do it my way and they never know if their way would have been better!"

As *Grand Hotel* edged closer to camera work, Paul Fejos, the first man in the studio to read the play, lost all chance to be its director. The film had become too important for a director whose previous directing credits were unimportant. When his name was struck from the list, he took it with good grace, but fled Hollywood for Europe.

Every one of the studio's staff directors confidently expected the invitation to make *Grand Hotel* would be tendered to one of them. It wasn't.

A party aspect began to surround the project when lighthearted, light-mannered, multitalented Edmund Goulding danced center stage, having been handed the plum.

Thalberg was influenced by a belief Goulding's homosexuality would bring new dimensions to the performance of Greta Garbo and Joan Crawford, and said so.

"Eddie thinks like a woman," he said. "He'll bring out their femininity. I want them to stand out over the men."

A composer who couldn't play a musical instrument but whistled his songs, Goulding was the creator of the classic tune, "Love, Your Magic Spell Is Everywhere." He was a writer who couldn't write, but told stories others had to put on paper for him. In that manner he wrote the first film Joan Crawford appeared in, *Sally, Irene and Mary,* combining characters from three successful Broadway musicals.

He was a breed common to Hollywood then, when stories were constantly needed to keep production lines rolling. He had a way of showing up with material to fill the void, a freelance specialist much like a doctor or lawyer whose timely appearance saved a life or a day, winning gratitude and financial rewards.

While the production department prepared *Grand Hotel,* Goulding waylaid Thalberg one morning and suggested a story that could be a captivating piece for Norma Shearer. Staff writer Gertrude Purcell was assigned to hear it from Goulding, who promised to tell it to her exactly as he had told it to Thalberg so she could put it on paper. It took her three weeks to make the transfer. When Thalberg read her work it didn't resemble anything he had ever heard, but by then he couldn't remember the story and neither could Goulding.

Grand Hotel started shooting December 31, 1930, an appropriate time for New Year revels. It was shot in exactly three weeks in January, so smoothly that it was completed and premiered April 17, 1931, at Grauman's Chinese Theatre on Hollywood Boulevard.

The theatre belonged to a famous Hollywood exhibitor, Sid Grauman, who wasn't unlike Goulding in ebullience of spirit. A gregarious, popular man-about-town, he was a personal friend of a majority of the men and women in the theatre that night. Before the show began, he came on stage and announced that he had persuaded Greta Garbo to break her rule and make an appearance after the film. It caused a wave of expectation, and the prospect of seeing the elusive star seemed to hang over the screening.

When the picture ended, the houselights went up. Grauman reappeared to announce "Miss Greta Garbo!" and then one of the film's stars, Wallace Beery, in a messy evening gown and unkempt blonde wig, pranced into view. The audience was stunned with disappointment.

On stage, Grauman shouted repeatedly that it was all a joke. His words were ignored as the audience headed silently for the exits.

With *Unholy Garden* finished and out of their typewriters, Hecht went home to Nyack, and MacArthur went to Thalberg. He wanted to rewrite the scenario of *Lullaby,* pleading that he could bring love and understanding to this important step in his wife's career and provide emotional values beyond the words of gifted Frances Marion. As a former reporter well-versed at meeting deadlines, he would deliver his work in three weeks, before the film's scheduled start date, May 12, 1931. Thalberg said, "Do it" and he did.

Thereupon, in what had become his annual rite of Spring, Thalberg took a break from his busy life-style. En route to a European vacation, he phoned his associates from New York, just before boarding an ocean liner. The call was made at lunchtime to the executive dining room. Among those present was Eastern story editor Bertram Bloch, who expressed astonishment at the conversation he was hearing. There was no talk of movies or movie making, just queries about Thalberg's health. Did he have warm clothing, raincoat, umbrella and plenty of medicines?

It was then that Hyman made the remark that impressed me so forcibly, "As long as Irving lives we're all great men!"

The MacArthur scenario of *Lullaby* rolled smoothly through its shooting schedule, directed by Edgar Selwyn, who had also put on the stage version years before. The machinery performed so smoothly that Selwyn called "Cut" to the cameraman June 2, 1931, completing the final shot only twenty-one days after first commanding the traditional, "Lights! Camera! Action!" Then the cutter assembled the footage, the music department scored it (with canned music recorded for other films) and it was previewed just ten days later in San Bernardino, sixty miles away.

It was a sneak preview, so-called because it was sneaked away from film-wise Hollywood folk to try out before an average audience. Those moviegoers were in the dark about what they were about to see, responding to a revolving searchlight on the theatre roof that signalled a new movie would be shown.

The sneak preview custom enabled the producers to sample audience reactions before the glossy niceties of the finished movie went into general release. They often drew such highly enthusiastic responses that the producer could emerge from the theatre in a glow of happiness. Then, with worries and tensions behind, workers who fought like cats and dogs through the making of the movie embraced and reminded each other that "All is forgiven when you have a good preview."

On the other side of that coin, however, audiences might emerge from a sneak preview seriously doubting the Hollywood adage that "Nobody sets out to make a bad picture."

At the sneak preview of *Lullaby,* the main title was greeted with silence, indicating nobody in that San Bernardino theatre knew the name of Helen Hayes. They rolled off into the street even as the opening scenes flashed on, and as the film continued to roll, so did they.

With Thalberg away, only Selwyn, Rapf, MacArthur and I made up the studio contingent. As we drove to "San Berdoo" in a studio limousine, Rapf ventured a prediction there wouldn't be a dry eye in the theatre when the movie was over. He was right, but there wasn't a wet one, either—the entire audience had departed long before "The End" appeared on the screen.

MacArthur was desolate. "Helen has been a star thirty years," he moaned, "and I've ruined her in one night!"

Heading away from the debacle, he curled up in the back seat of the car, his sunny disposition in eclipse.

Passing a village drugstore, he shouted "Stop" to the driver, then leaped out of the car and ran into it. A thought occurred. Drugstores sold bichloride of mercury, a popular pill for suicides. In a kind of morbid flashback I recalled that Charlie was an aficionado of involuntary exits from life. There is an attempted suicide in his play *The Front Page,* and he once recalled covering a hanging where a condemned killer, standing at the foot of a shakily-erected gallows, asked, "Is this thing safe?"

I raced after him, but he wasn't at the drug counter, he was in the phone booth, talking vehemently behind the glass door. He emerged shouting, "The Marines have landed!" Ben Hecht was coming west to help him rescue *Lullaby.*

Helen Hayes took her husband's account of the preview with philosophic calm, comforted by Charlie's confidence that Hecht would help him make the film well.

Bad preview reactions always spawned excuses. Producers were certain their movie had the bad luck to be shown to the wrong audience. The same film that had no appeal to workers in the fruit belt might appeal to big town intellectuals. All producers always hoped those hopes, but for *Lullaby* the sorry verdict of San Bernardino was upheld wherever the film was shown.

Hecht arrived with a companion—an attractive redhead. Lady Hamilton, as he called her, was a wonderful secretary. He was so fearful of losing her they shared the same room in the MacArthur menage so he could protect her from predatory movie moguls. A skeptical Helen Hayes promptly took her child and checked into the Santa Barbara Biltmore, one hundred miles north of the action.

On the 4th of July, fireworks lit up the skies. Producer Samuel Goldwyn chose a theatre facing the beach at Santa Monica for a sneak preview of *The Unholy Garden*. It, too, was an unmitigated disaster. Director George Fitzmaurice talked of walking into the ocean, but was restrained.

Jed Harris was still very much in evidence on the California scene, fanatically eager to get a third act for *Twentieth Century*. He and Goldwyn were waylaying Hecht and MacArthur night and day, seeking remedies for their crippled products.

To MacArthur, the plight of *Lullaby* was the true urgency, but he was unable to get Hecht to settle down and work for him. Enamored of Mrs. Hamilton, coauthor Hecht took her sightseeing, promising only that he would settle down after the lady had enough of the delights of southern California.

The month of July 1931 heaped thirty-one black days on the sunny character of Charles MacArthur. He was waiting at the studio gate on August 1, when Thalberg returned.

After a poignant recitation from a subdued MacArthur, the studio head viewed *Lullaby* alone, behind a locked door in his studio projection room. When he emerged, he shocked the writer with his first suggestion: "Send Hecht home." He offered in exchange to reshoot every frame of the film if that became necessary to turn it into a hit.

Hecht was unwilling to return east without MacArthur because Jed Harris was such a persistent problem, so getting rid of him required inspiration. MacArthur told Jed Harris the three of them would train out together. Ticket arrangements were made, bags were packed, cars arrived to take them away.

But MacArthur wasn't at the Hacienda. Instead, he sent a message he would catch the train during its five-minute stop-over at Pasadena.

He was there, just as he said he would be, but roaring drunk and accompanied by Dr. Sam Hirschfield, who was Hecht's medical idol. Doctor Sam told Ben that Charlie was a desperately sick man. He insisted he must stay in his care until he was completely sober.

Hecht didn't realize it was an act until he was back in Nyack, when Charlie called and confessed it was just a performance. Hecht congratulated his writing partner for contributing a new anecdote to their history but castigated Dr. Hirschfield saying, "He wasted a hell of a lot of time running errands for fools and ingrates!"

During the twenty-one days of retakes, duplicating the original shooting schedule, my department was asked to supply a new title for *Lullaby,* already tarnished with gossiped reports it was a sure flop.

To find a new title, it was routine for my department to circulate a request to the writers, readers and other interested studio workers. Included was a thumbnail sketch of the story and an offer of fifty dollars to the winner. The memorandum outlined the plot of the film as a tearful tale of a prostitute's sacrifice and struggle to help her illegitimate son to manhood. Staff writer A. P. Younger suggested it be called *Son of a Bitch.* He didn't win. *The Sin of Madelon Claudet* did and under that name, the film achieved hit status.

By 1932 I was making trips east to prospect for stories, always with a stopover in Philadelphia to visit the editorial gang at the *Saturday Evening Post*. The magazine ran the most popular fiction appearing anywhere in the country and, while agents often sent the studio manuscripts as yet unpublished, there was always a chance I could ferret out some nuggets nobody had seen. It was during one of those explorations that I heard about an upcoming serial with exciting movie possibilities— *Red-Headed Woman,* by Katharine Brush. Its screen adaptation would involve a long-time favorite of mine—a bit tarnished, a bit faded, a bit desperate—but truly a full-fledged legend.

The first chapters gave evidence that its principal character was made to order for F. Scott Fitzgerald. A sexy beauty's journey from the wrong side of the tracks to the right side of rich men's beds was an amusing portrayal that easily could have been titled after one of his books, *The Beautiful and the Damned.* Thalberg agreed enthusiastically with the choice of Fitzgerald and arrangements for him to script the story were swiftly made, so swiftly in fact that he would have to stay on hold back home in Baltimore until we could get the complete manuscript, which was still nonexistent.

The *Post* broke its rule not to start serializing a story until the author finished it. Katherine Brush had come through at the last minute with her previous book and they took her word she would bring in the complete *Red-Headed Woman* in time. I left Philadelphia and headed for a meeting with her at her residence on the twelfth floor of an impressive apartment building in midtown Manhattan, close by the East River.

The front door was vivid red with chromium knobs, opening onto a huge living room, high-ceilinged, with fifteen-foot windows. A garret, yes, but no Bohemian squalor for this struggling author.

Only two chairs and a couch furnished the wide expanse of floor. The lack of clutter was too noticeable to ignore; I lied and said I liked the decor and she seemed pleased. I found out later that the wide-open spaces were due to her husband going broke in the stock-market. Their combined income wasn't sufficient to let them buy enough furniture to suit their tastes.

A stunning redhead, Katherine Brush was the most stylish lady writer I ever met. She was also incredibly truthful. We got right down to the basics of *Red-Headed Woman*.

"How will you end it?" I asked.

"Your guess is as good as mine."

She went on to say that she always started stories without knowing how to end them. "When I sell one I give myself a deadline and find a way out. So, don't worry."

Actually, I didn't, as I assumed that some editor of the *Post* would worry enough for the two of us.

She was delighted that Fitzgerald would do the scenario, recalling that when she started writing, she "sedulously aped his style" and said she was disappointed when reviewers of her work failed to notice it.

Red-Headed Woman was assigned to supervisor Paul Bern, whose erudition qualified him to bring out the rampant sex Miss Brush's story zeroed in on. To hurry along its film presentation and cash in on the popularity of the serialization, still running nicely ahead of Katherine Brush's imagination, Fitzgerald was summoned to Hollywood.

Scott's contract required the studio to provide living quarters during his stay. We rented a penthouse at a Hollywood Boulevard hotel and director King Vidor, a friend of the author, arranged to dine with us the night of Fitzgerald's arrival.

"Then you won't need a formal introduction when he comes to the studio," said Vidor, and I eagerly assented.

The term *alcoholic* wasn't used then. The heavy drinker was a drunkard, a lush, a souse, his fate was a matter between him and God. There were no detoxification centers, no therapists available in hospitals, no learned explanations that drunkenness was due to a chemical imbalance. If the inebriate went looking for sympathy or a cure, he would probably talk it over with a psychiatrist and the matter would have remained secret. At this time in Fitzgerald's life, his wife Zelda was in a sanitarium with severe mental problems and he was reputed to have kicked the drinking habit he had notoriously acquired in his formative years.

Marie and I arrived eagerly for our dinner date. With the admiration for him I had developed when I read *This Side of Paradise,* I hardly needed an introduction. He had a built-in class and style and we fell into instant friendship, as I knew we would.

Handsome as his earliest photographs, with his well-known peach-blossom complexion and male-model look, Fitzgerald talked knowledgeably about the demands of screen writing and how he was sure he could meet them. When I spoke of my enjoyment of *This Side of Paradise,* he quipped that he would change the name of the principal character from Amory to Samory in the next edition. He hoisted his glass.

He took one sip and his eyes glazed, his speech slurred. Whatever the cause, scientific or not, one drink was one too many. He couldn't rise from his chair. Marie and I dined alone with the Vidors, a rather sad and reflective foursome.

In their first story conference, Thalberg and Bern spoke of their concept of *Red-Headed Woman.* They wanted it to have the viewpoint of a whirlwind female who thoroughly enjoyed her way with men.

"We have to laugh *with* her, not *at* her," they told Fitzgerald.

Six weeks later, he finished the job and turned it in. I put the machinery in motion to get him his final paycheck and transportation back to Baltimore. He was elated with his work. His previous Hollywood writings had landed on the shelves of the unproduced, abandoned orphans that left black and in-eradicable marks against their creator. *Red-Headed Woman* looked to be the upward turn for the fabulous career that had somehow fallen flat.

Paul Bern had already engaged a gregarious Balkan, Marcel de Sano, to direct Fitzgerald's script. His previous work was a silent movie assignment five years before, an Irish period comedy. He, too, looked on *Red-Headed Woman* as the comeback movie he needed and stayed close to the author while he wrote the final pages of the scenario.

He influenced Fitzgerald to slant scenes to fit his directorial ideas. Scott was eager to please all comers and his spirits (the mental kind) were lifted sky-high when Thalberg and Bern praised his work and wished him a speedy journey home.

But their praise was staged.

"He didn't grasp the point about laughing *with* her," mourned Thalberg and, still trying to cash in quickly on the now-completed serialization, assigned Anita Loos to start over.

Everyone knew this disappointment would be a shattering blow to Fitzgerald and a plan to avoid a catastrophe was devised. All concerned were asked to keep developments secret until he returned home when a detailed letter would explain it. It was a deceitful plot devised for the benefit of the deceived. My role was to deliver his check and train ticket to his hotel. But he suddenly showed up at the studio, wanting to say goodbye in person to everyone he knew.

He toured the offices for an hour, unsuspecting and oblivious, while all the people he met acted out the false front. He was just leaving when director de Sano was coming in and maliciously told him he had been tricked. "Anita Loos is starting over from the beginning." With that, Fitzgerald took off on a monumental drunk and Thalberg fired de Sano.

Tiny Anita Loos was a towering screen writer. Four-feet, eleven-inches small and only ninety pounds, she had begun writing movies at eighteen. By forty, as she was then, there could be no accurate count of her screenplays. She admitted that even her own guess would surely fall short.

She had no problem understanding the concept of laughing with a character, proving it with Lorelei Lee in her best-known book, *Gentlemen Prefer Blondes*. It was Anita's monument, eclipsing everything else she wrote, an international best-seller that would also be a play, a musical comedy, and two movies. *Gentlemen Prefer Blondes* became a byword in many languages. Anita laughed privately at it for she was forever a brunette.

Her jet-black locks were barbered in a straight cut that hung over her forehead, patterned after a newspaper cartoon character, Buster Brown. Sometimes a tiny beret perched on top of her head, or a Panama hat hung back of center with streaming ribbons. Her regular attire was a dark blue sailor suit with the skirt short at the knees, giving the perfect illusion of an innocent little girl-child. Behind that image was one of the sexiest laugh-makers ever to sprinkle dialogue with bawdy innuendoes.

Anita's life held many deceptions. Her little-girl look was heightened by the way she held onto the hand of John Emerson, her constant escort. To strangers they appeared to be a father and daughter, for he was at least twenty years older. During fourteen years of collaborations his name appeared ahead of hers on the credits of more than thirty films. But they were man and wife and all the writing was hers. His career as a director had faded away and Anita helped him keep his self-respect with the shared credits.

A hard worker in the mornings, Anita parked her labors in her desk drawer at noon and sallied forth for an arm-in-arm stroll with her pals on the lot, humorists all—Robert Benchley, Donald Ogden Stewart, Charlie MacArthur and Bob Hopkins.

Hopkins, popularly known as Hoppy, carried a cup of black coffee and spewed out words like machine gun bullets. His speaking style of jerky sentences was punctuated by the use of his free hand to poke the side or stomach of the closest person. A master of insults, his companions were common targets. "What's all this crap about making heroes? Who needs heroes in this fucking business? I can make a snake a hero. The villain grabs the girl's tits and the snake stings him in the ass. Audience cheers, the snake's a hero. Get it? Only business in the world that can make a fucking snake a hero. What's with you jerks? Y'don't get it?"

Knowing he was easily insulted by rejection, Benchley, Loos, Stewart and MacArthur assumed baffled expressions and the affronted gag man would gulp the remains of his coffee and stride away, muttering. Next day he would be back with a repeat performance on another subject.

A literary reactionary and reputed fire-eater, Upton Sinclair made news long before Marie and I moved to Hollywood. Many of his books were best-sellers, their titles revealing the themes he preferred and the fervor he poured into them: *The Jungle; The Moneychangers; Cry for Justice; King Coal*, subtitled *A Novel of the Colorado Strike; Oil!;* and *The Goose-Step*, subtitled *A Study in American Education.* He had more than thirty books in circulation when he contacted me from his Pasadena home to urge consideration of the movie possibilities in his just-completed novel, *The Wet Parade,* about the current Prohibition Act that banned the sale of alcoholic liquors. He offered to bring the manuscript to my office.

The Eighteenth Amendment, outlawing strong drink in the United States, was a bonanza for the movie business. The law spawned bootleggers, speakeasies and violence—three colorful ingredients for action films. Sinclair assured me his book had these and more, which certainly made it worthy of scrutiny. As public opinion strongly favored repeal, it hardly mattered which side Sinclair was on, it was a foregone conclusion this Congressional error in judgment would soon be corrected.

When I mentioned that I had an appointment with Sinclair, I was totally unprepared for Thalberg's opposition. He said, "Don't let that Bolshevik inside this studio!"

But he hadn't said the new book was taboo, so I invited the author to bring his wife and the manuscript to dinner in our new apartment. Like many New Yorkers accustomed to apartment living, we never noticed the "For Sale" signs dotting the lawns of depressed southern California homes. Instead, we rented space in a garish new building in Hollywood, near legendary Sunset Boulevard. It was on the fourth floor, which was as high as we could get, and you could imagine the Great White Way when you looked out the window because there were some bright lights in view. It wasn't Broadway and it wasn't Manhattan, but it was home.

Because of Thalberg's reaction, I awaited Sinclair rather tremulously, deciding to greet him in the courtyard and make a quick decision about spending an entire evening with a famous social activist.

I was unprepared for the charming, slender gray-haired gentleman. He observed the dazzling facade of the apartment structure into which I was now guiding him, drew himself up majestically, and made like King Arthur as, with a sweep of an imaginary sword, he solemnly proclaimed, "I dub thee Platinum Blonde!"

Sinclair and I soon became pen pals. He was a nonstop letter writer, ceaselessly pitching ideas for movies or asking consideration for friends he felt would add value to the making of motion pictures. It was obvious, however, the years had cooled some of his ardor for change. *The Wet Parade* took no sides for or against Prohibition, a weakness that hurt some of its power as a motion picture. (Thalberg did buy the right to film it, but constantly reminded me the "Bolshevik" was not to come inside the walls.)

Negotiations were conducted at Sinclair's home in Pasadena, and went on for some weeks. Even as our friendly deal for Upton Sinclair's *The Wet Parade* was being structured, letters from the author poured in. This one was typical:

Mr. Sam Marx
Metro-Goldwyn-Mayer
Culver City, California

Dear Sam:
I enclose a copy of The Machine *about which we talked over the phone. You might find the basis for a timely picture in it—despite the fact that it was written nearly twenty-five years ago.*

Also, I want to ask you whether you have ever read my novel, Manassas? *Thalberg had in mind an*

American Calvacade, and it occurred to me that
Manassas might be a basis for such a historical picture.
It is a story of the years preceding the Civil War, and
takes in many historical episodes. Jack London called
it "The best Civil War story I have read," and many
people still consider it my best novel. It was to be a
trilogy, taking in the entire Civil War. If you want to
make a picture of it I could expand the story along the
lines of what I had in mind.

Sincerely,
U Sinclair

Finally, the papers were completed by the studio's legal department, transferring the rights to *The Wet Parade* forever and ever into eternity in the cold terminology that only lawyers love. I took turns reading it aloud with Mr. and Mrs. Sinclair in their parlor, translating its meanings as best we could in periodic discussions fortified by strong cups of hot tea. In those relaxed moments I stressed Thalberg's desire for finer films.

I was caught off guard when Mrs. Sinclair asked if some adherence to the integrity of her husband's book might be written into the contract. I was sure it could be.

To save time—and another trip to Pasadena—we wrote on the margin of the contract that the studio would make every possible effort to maintain the intent of the novel. I initialed the newly penned line and so did Sinclair. Then I handed him a check for twenty-five thousand dollars. The deal was concluded.

Concluded, that is, until about ten minutes after I returned to the studio and delivered the contract to the legal department. The inter-office-communication gadget on my desk buzzed and Thalberg's voice issued through it in harsher tones than I had ever heard.

"Come up here," he barked.

He was standing by his desk, white with rage, clutching the rolled-up contract.

"What do you mean changing this?" he demanded. "Who do you think you are? Who gave you the authority? I'm a Vice-President of this company, I'm in charge of production but I never change a word in a contract!"

There was no sense explaining it was due to praising him. Naiveté was no excuse; I was guilty, as charged, of an act of incredible stupidity. Given Thalberg's abhorrence of the man to begin with, it would have been useless to plead that the warmth and friendliness of the Sinclairs had beguiled me.

He stormed up and down his office, his voice hoarse with frustration. "Thanks to you he can take us to court and prevent our showing the film. He can say we did not maintain the intent of his book after we've spent a million dollars and Sinclair is just the man to do it."

He was interrupted by a long-distance phone call, whereupon he ordered me to wait in the anteroom. I seized this reprieve to phone Sinclair in Pasadena and tell him what was happening to me. He seemed quite unconcerned, saying it sounded as though the studio really didn't care to maintain the intent of his work. Then Thalberg flung open the door and commanded that I return to his office.

He picked up the tirade as if there had been no interruption. His theme was that I was giving myself unwarranted importance, and though I was not an officer of this Hundred Million Dollar corporation I had placed its assets in jeopardy. He enlarged on the idea that "that Pasadena Bolshevik" could sue for tremendous damages.

He flung the contract into the wastebasket. "I won't make the picture!"

A second interruption came when Thalberg's secretary announced on her intercom that Upton Sinclair was calling him from Pasadena. The conversation was brief. Mr. and Mrs. Sinclair felt that the sentence in the margin of the contract might have a salutary effect on the filming of the novel, but if it caused any distress to the studio they were quite agreeable that Thalberg strike it out. Mr. Sinclair would put a letter in the mail verifying this.

Thalberg hung up the phone, and said mildly, "Don't you ever do that again."

I returned limply to my office.

The film turned out well, and I brought the Sinclairs to the studio to see it and they liked it very much. I also brought them to Thalberg's office and introduced them. It was a short meeting. While shaking hands, Mrs. Sinclair asked Thalberg if he was the one they called the Boy Wonder. He stared coldly at her and said, "If so, I never heard it." They left. The studio continued to stand up just fine, all in one piece, despite the visit of "that Bolshevik."

Chapter Seven

Although she showed little interest in the crusades of Upton Sinclair, Kate Corbaley also had a deeply ingrained anger against injustice and was more willing than I to deal with social problems.

In our story meetings, Thalberg was always quick to spot messages. Not that it was hard to catch their drift—few writers dealt lightly with parlous times. Their themes were as downbeat as their sources and tended to erupt in tragedy. Thalberg preferred happy endings, but listened to sad conclusions if, as he said, "The ending is what the beginning is about."

Louis B. Mayer never read books but he loved to listen to stories and admired Corbaley's gift of narrative. His office door was always open to her and, at times, when she was determined to get a thorough hearing for a yarn she liked, she would take it to him. But he had a low tolerance for sad movies and in rejecting one of her favorites told her, "Tragedy is death at the box office."

Thalberg laughed when he heard it but said he concurred.

He laughed again when company president Nicholas M. Schenck was quoted in the trade papers as saying, "There's nothing wrong with this business that a good picture won't cure."

Thalberg was constantly scornful of the top boss, whose toughminded fiscal management clashed with his own toughminded creative management. "He thinks we're a bunch of bad boys who make bad pictures just to annoy him, and he wants us to stop."

There was no sign of antagonism on the social surface when Schenck made one of his periodic visits to the West Coast. Marie and I were invited to a dinner-dance in his honor at the Beverly Hills home of director Edgar Selwyn. Called "The General" by his intimates, Schenck was a chunky individual whose body looked carved from granite. He had just inherited the company's pinnacle position from its recently deceased founding father, Marcus Loew.

On this occasion, Schenck's wife Pansy, a small, attractive and demure woman, accompanied him. She was the sister of Selwyn's wife, former Broadway actress Ruth Wilcox, a flaming redhead with a spectacular flair for calling attention to herself. The two couples stood as a receiving line near the entrance to the house, where Edgar Selwyn introduced us. It was my first meeting with "The General," who had evidently been briefed about me. He shook my hand warmly, then spoke with a deep, guttural accent.

"I hope you will find for me more stories for free like *Grand Hotel.*" I gulped at the sheer impossibility that I or anyone else could ever duplicate that feat, but recovered enough to assure him I would do my best. Then I headed for the bar to reflect on the naiveté of the company president.

After dinner I was recruited for a bridge game, and when I went to tell Marie, I had to break in on an animated conversation she was having with Walt Disney, the unrivalled genius of cartoons. A vision of Rudolf Friml at the Wodehouse party flashed through my mind, for she took little notice of what I said and, when I left, she and Disney resumed their dialogue. On our way home, at three in the morning, I admitted some curiosity about her Disney discussion. Was he, perhaps, suggesting they take off for some far-flung outpost to rendezvous with Mickey Mouse or Donald Duck?

"He wasn't the least bit interested in me or what I was saying," she said with some exasperation. She pointed to the designer-made hook at the neck of her evening dress. There were two caricaturish figures resembling swollen blowfish, faces close as though kissing, holding the top of her gown closed.

"Mr. Disney wasn't listening to a word I said," she explained. "He was just studying these fish!"

When I drifted into the studio next morning, screen writer F. Hugh Herbert was waiting for me. A survivor of the silent era, he had such a deep love for MGM that, when he married, he asked for and received permission to have the ceremony performed in a churchlike set on the back lot of the studio. Considerable success as a playwright lay ahead for Hughie Herbert, but at this time I had him tabbed only as a serviceable freelance scenarist who could be called upon to assist newly arrived authors master the intricacies of scripting talkies.

The late-night festivities had left me sleepless and grumpy, and I suggested we postpone whatever it was he had on his mind.

"But I need a job, and Irving suggested I come see you this morning," he said.

"When did he do that?"

"Last night. He dropped in to see me at my house."

I ushered him into my office. "How do you feel, Hughie? Are you okay?"

"You think I made it up?"

"Yes, but with reason. How was he dressed?"

"In a tuxedo."

"And does he usually dress like that when he drops in on you?"

"I'll tell you exactly what happened. It was around ten o'clock. I was getting ready for bed when the doorbell rang. I went downstairs and it was Irving Thalberg. His car was at the curb. I invited him in and brought out some brandy and we sat down in the dining room. He asked me if I was working, and when I told him no, he said to go see you and ask if there's an assignment you can give me."

Although I was still skeptical, I recalled hearing Eddie Mannix tell a group of heavy gamblers at the next table, "Irving has a long-distance call. He wants us to start our game without him and he'll cut in when he's free." Then I remembered that it was at least an hour before Thalberg joined them.

Herbert finished his narrative, saying "When I woke up this morning, I thought I dreamt it, so I went downstairs and there was the brandy bottle, with two glasses, on the dining room table."

I saw Thalberg, as usual, in the late afternoon to discuss stories and writers.

"By the way," I said, "Hugh Herbert was waiting for me this morning. He said you told him to see me."

He gazed speculatively at me, then nodded. "I went to see someone who lives on the same street, but I rang the wrong doorbell. He asked me in and I couldn't refuse."

It seemed odd he didn't explain what happened and go on to his planned destination, but I saw no reason to press that point. "Hughie's not a bad writer," said Thalberg. "See if you can find something for him."

When I found something, it was an original story by F. Hugh Herbert, which Thalberg approved buying. It made an average program picture titled *The Woman in His Life*.

Most movies of life in America featured sweetness and light, with wedding bells at the end of every romantic path. Foreign writers took a more realistic approach to life, their submissions increasingly grim and dour as economic depression spread around the world. With my agreement, Corbaley continued to bring their stories to our meetings until, finally, we hit paydirt.

Eskimo depicted the rugged life of natives in the far north, its hero a family man and resourceful provider turned into a hunted criminal by events he could not control. It was a saga of heroism familiar to men whether they trudged the frozen tundra of the Polar regions or the hard cement of New York streets. The similarity of human drama, wherever it took place, usually went unnoticed by the supervisors although it had the attention of Mrs. Corbaley and myself. Because of our jobs, we were more aware of the limited number of plots that so many books and plays turned on, and how they could be recycled with different backgrounds.

The purchase of the film rights to *Eskimo* included a writing deal for its author and that brought Peter Freuchen from Denmark to Culver City. Accustomed to finding his way across trackless snow, it didn't occur to him to ask ahead for a guide. He walked up to the gate on a morning when a company shooting on the lot had an open call for tall, bearded men to play pirate types. Freuchen was six-foot-seven, with luxurious foliage on his face hiding the scars of many frostbites. Before he could identify himself, he was whisked off to the wardrobe department, given a pirate outfit and directed to report to the back lot. He had been told to expect surprises in Hollywood, so he was unfazed by this welcome and in fact, spent the morning on the set delighted by the goings-on around him. "I thought this was the way you welcome all your writers here," he said later that day, knowing it wasn't but loving the humor of it.

He finally ambled into my office after he found something else that delighted him even more than the movie set. The Boston baked beans in the commissary were the tastiest he had ever known. His experience with numberless cans of the stuff qualified him as an expert and he gorged himself daily on beans all his months at the studio.

Director Woody Van Dyke was an expert, too. His specialty was the making of films on far-off tropical locations. They included *White Shadows in the South Seas* and *Trader Horn.* He was a natural choice for *Eskimo,* but nothing he had handled before required the time and attention Freuchen's epic tale demanded. It was a full year in preparation. During that time the huge black-bearded Dane became a one-man legend as he assisted everyone on its preproduction, relating adventures with twinkling eyes, knowing nobody could deny their truth, then reacting to his own stories with a great booming laugh.

Freuchen couldn't dissuade Van Dyke from stocking unusable items like, for example, an electric refrigerator.

"If you want ice I can chop it for you at the place where you are standing," Freuchen told him.

Van Dyke enjoyed gin for breakfast and suffered miserably

in Tahiti and Africa when forced to imbibe warm martinis. It was joked around the studio that he had refused to go to earthquake-ridden New Zealand because he liked his Bloody Marys stirred, not shaken.

Before turning to writing, Freuchen was a meterologist in Greenland and governor of a colony of Eskimos, learning their language and marrying one of their women. At an early age he studied medicine, according to one of his anecdotes.

"I attended to this young feller badly hurt by an accident," he said. "My colleagues gave up hope of saving him but I decided to try. It was a tough job. I lived by his bed until he pulled through and finally the day came that he could go home. Very proudly, I watched from a window in the hospital. When he started across the street I saw him hit by a car and killed. That minute I decided not to fight God's wishes. I quit the hospital and went to sea."

He claimed he had cut off his own leg when gangrene set in while he wintered in an ice cave. The wooden leg that helped support his great bulk attested to the loss of that limb even if it didn't prove it happened as he told it.

He was the embodiment of a fine storyteller and those studio associates who doubted his veracity often found reason to doubt their own doubts.

He was unhappy when the production office decided *Eskimo* should be filmed in Alaska instead of Greenland, which was the locale of his book. They brushed aside his views on the desirability of Greenland. A location scout persuaded them that a recently found passage into Alaska made it the most accessible locale. To win this point, he picked up a book and started to read aloud about the new way to the northwest. To his surprise, the first paragraph stated that the passage was discovered by Danish explorer Peter Freuchen.

Eskimo went to Alaska.

While Freuchen was there, international financier Ivar Kreuger, known as the Match King, committed suicide, causing the collapse of his financial empire.

Freuchen wrote me from Teller, Alaska, "I hear you are going to make a picture about the Match King Kreuger. For God's sake wait until I am back and let me play one of the stockholders. I can do it without make-up. I know how it feels and I can get the feeling back any second. All that I make now goes to pay what I lost from him. He was my friend. Nice boy. Therefore, I wish Mr. Thalberg had been intelligent enough to realize that I deserve more money. But I agree with him, he and I are too great men to argue about such low material as money."

Money didn't seem to be on the mind of the next newcomer.

"I want to write for Mickey Mouse."

The quiet stranger was very serious. I told him Mickey was under contract elsewhere and would be difficult to borrow.

It was early May 1932. Thirty-four-year-old William Faulkner had shown up a week later than his contract date. Then he walked up to a studio guard and asked to see the person who looked after writers.

Shy-mannered, with close-cropped iron gray hair and an inconspicuous black mustache, he wore a rumpled brown tweed jacket and unpressed khaki pants, also inconspicuous. The only conspicuous thing about him was a blood-caked bruise on his forehead.

"I was in a taxi accident in New Orleans."

He didn't like New Orleans. "Too big." He felt the same about Los Angeles. "Bigger," he said laconically.

He didn't want a wrestling tale, an assignment that had already been determined for him.

"I came here to work on my own ideas."

He spoke with the inflection of the typical courtly southerner although pitched a trifle higher than one expected. He was alternatively defensive and defiant.

"Why don't I write newsreels for you? Newsreels and Mickey Mouse are the only movies I like." But like Mickey, newsreels hardly required the services of this rising figure in American literary circles.

"We'd prefer to assign you to a wrestling yarn for Wally Beery."

"Who's he?"

The best answer would be to show him the star's work. His latest film was a perfect example. Beery's popularity always climbed when he protrayed a snivelling slob. The role of the wrestler was to be an extension of the boxer he played in his newest success, *The Champ*. Its elements were exact. In movie studios, imitation was more than a pure form of flattery, it was also a pure form of sequel.

A studio messenger was called to accompany Faulkner to a projection room. I told the boy to sit through the movie and answer all questions. They went off and I phoned Faulkner's agent, Leland Hayward, in his Beverly Hills headquarters and told him his errant author had appeared. He said he would come right over.

The messenger boy came back first.

"He's gone," he reported. "He didn't want to hear about Wally, he only wanted to talk about dogs. He said I should be ashamed not to own a dog and so should everybody else who doesn't own a dog.

"As soon as the picture started he asked me, 'How do you stop this thing?' He said there was no use looking at it because he knew how it would come out. I tried to explain he was to watch Wally but then he asked, 'How do I get out of here?' so I showed him and he went."

At this point, Leland Hayward arrived in breathless pursuit of his client. He was too late, Faulkner had disappeared again. The wrestling yarn for Beery was assigned to another newcomer from the east, Moss Hart.

Three weeks later, Faulkner appeared again. He had been wandering Death Valley, steeling himself to work in the great gray walls of the overpowering studio in enormous Los Angeles.

He was ready, then, to work on other than newsreels and Mickey Mouse. But word of his antics had been magnified to the supervisors who were wary of all writers believed to be eccentrics.

Faulkner sat in his office every day and practiced writing original scenarios, all of which found their way into the studio archives but none onto the screen. While he labored, his fame and the world's esteem for his writing continued to grow.

Danish character actor Jean Hersholt asked me to help him get Faulkner's autograph. I arranged a meeting in my office, and the actor arrived with a dozen leather-bound volumes in his arms, so heavy he could barely carry them. Many authors might be flattered by such a display; Faulkner looked at Hersholt coldly and said, "Pick out the one you like best and I'll sign it." I watched as Hersholt appraised his collection a long time and then selected *Sanctuary.*

Wallace Beery played his usual part in the wrestling film. After Faulkner walked out, it was assigned to Moss Hart by default, imperfect material for the gifted and debonair playwright from Manhattan. But that didn't bother him; he tried hard to make it work. Eager to be a part of the Hollywood writing fraternity, he realized his ambition admirably as the years went on. In that sense, being assigned to "flesh" worked to Hart's advantage. It was such an ordinary yarn that, as a first-time exercise in screen writing, he had nowhere else to go but up.

Moss and I met earlier when he came to Los Angeles as an actor, portraying a screen writer in the touring company of his first play, *Once in a Lifetime.* His collaborator, George S. Kaufman, acted it during its Broadway run.

It wasn't what you might call a demanding role. The character merely sat in the outer office of a studio boss waiting to see him. In that scene in the play, a studio messenger would appear periodically carrying a sign announcing, "Mr. Glogauer is on Number Two" or some other stage and Moss would react. Moss loved doing it.

He had a fabulous enthusiasm for show business and a high quotient of hero worship. Thalberg was one of his idols and I set up an appointment for them to meet on a nonmatinee afternoon. It led to a little joke that originated in the impish mind of writer Charley Lederer.

We escorted Hart to Thalberg's outer office as planned. A secretary informed us the studio head was not in his office, so we sat down to wait. Then a boy, grotesquely uniformed by the wardrobe department, came in with a sign, prepared by the prop department, that read, "Mr. Thalberg is on Number Thirteen." This went on past the time we had allotted. The gag went sour. Thalberg was really out on a stage and didn't get back before the actor-playwright had to get to the theatre.

I should have known Charley Lederer's joke would fail. It happened to all his exploits. This bright young writer, wildly enamored of Hecht and MacArthur's zany doings, was constantly trying to duplicate them in some way that would bear telling in the literary gatherings around town. But they never worked out in the way he planned.

One of Lederer's misadventures began with a phone conversation to a girl who lived just around the corner. When she told him she was going out soon, he ran full speed to her front door and threw himself in the gutter, wanting her to find him lying there when she came out. He expected her to scream and carry on hysterically. But before she came out, a car ran over his arm.

Lederer spun giddily in Hollywood's best social circles, a joyful and gregarious soul. He held the key to invitations to the fabulous Hearst Ranch through his aunt, Marion Davies, beloved of the newspaper tycoon who also produced her films. Invitations to the ranch were greatly desired and many studio executives esteemed Lederer's social connections while denigrating his creative talents. He knew it and shrugged it off, content to bask in the glorious shadow of his idol, Ben Hecht. Lederer's reverence for the writer was welcomed by Hecht, not just to satisfy Hecht's ego but also for tax reasons. The income from books, plays and films didn't bring in enough money to finance this magnificent *bon vivant*. Hiding the costs of incessant hanky-panky, which he hugely enjoyed and claimed necessary to stimulate his writing, was impossible to explain to his wife and the Internal Revenue Service. Fortunately for Ben, Mrs. Rosie Hecht remained grounded full-time at their Nyack-on-the-Hudson home with an unruly daughter, enabling Ben to travel the world with other females. To finance these *sub-rosa* adventures, a phrase that in this case enjoyed a double meaning, agent Leland Hayward sought assignments for Hecht that Lederer could ghostwrite for small compensations he called "Sweet Nosegays and Personal Glory," while Hecht snared the major share of the cash and the credits.

In its four years of existence, the Academy of Motion Picture Arts and Sciences handed out its awards for excellence every autumn. Its members voted for the best films they had seen the previous winter and spring seasons. Successful nominees were notified by the Board of Directors when they won. But for the years 1931–32, a huge party would celebrate the event. The Academy Awards had become an occasion.

The elite of the industry gathered for that party November 18, 1932, at the Cocoanut Grove in the Ambassador Hotel. It was one week after Franklin D. Roosevelt had defeated Herbert Hoover for the presidency of the troubled United States.

MGM had four of the eight films vying for assorted honors from the Academy that year and with each attracting personal devotees, it tended to dilute all their chances. For best actress, Helen Hayes had to contend with another important Broadway star making her film debut, Lynn Fontanne in *The Guardsman.*

Waiting for the decisions to be announced, the members held a party that mixed a rowdy combination of industry prosperity and political nervousness. Then, *Grand Hotel* was declared Best Picture of the Year and Helen Hayes took home an Oscar for her portrayal of Madelon Claudet.

Chapter Eight

Thalberg was displaying a nervous restlessness that manifested itself when he began to flip a twenty-dollar gold piece during story conferences in his office. He sent the heavy coin twisting upward in somersault motions, catching and repeating it time after time until one day, to his surprise, it didn't come down to his outstretched palm. He had flipped it into the chandelier.

With that, he took to bouncing it hard on his glass-topped desk and catching it on the fly. The crash of gold on glass severely distracted his conferees and a group of uneasy associates decided to show him how it sounded. We armed ourselves with similar gold pieces and when he started bouncing his, we produced ours and stood around the desk, all bouncing gold pieces with him. It was a fun lesson and an instant cure, but even breaking that habit didn't disguise the fact that the studio boss was showing strain.

On December 24, 1932, five weeks after the Academy Awards, the studio celebrated the coming of Christmas with a fantastic party. Barriers tumbled down as workers *en masse* paraded through stages and offices. Messenger boys linked arms with directors, stars with secretaries, janitors with executives. Kisses and embraces were exchanged in a monumental show of unrefined joy. The resident bootleggers got so drunk they wandered the lot giving away their wares all over the lot. Charlie MacArthur, living in a bungalow on the grounds of the Beverly Hills Hotel, claimed he woke up next day naked in his bed with no recollection how he got there, his underwear and outerwear hanging on branches of a distant palm tree.

In the studio's projection rooms, pornographic movies enjoyed nonstop screening to the delectation of the roving celebrants. An increasing number of locked doors in the later hours indicated boys and girls were turning screen fantasies into stark realism.

Thalberg was the target of all celebrants still ambulatory and he joined in all their toasts to the company's continued success. Riding a high of personal satisfaction, he hoisted too many glasses, and barely made it home before he was felled by a massive heart attack.

By New Year's Day, the highlights of that party were dimmed when the news of Thalberg's collapse became known. He was to be out of action for an indefinite period. The studio became like a great ship that lost its rudder and the power to move ahead.

The door to the executive's sickroom was barred by his wife, who acted on doctor's orders and turned away all who called. However, she divulged that the heart attack may not have been as serious as first diagnosed, as the medics believed his long-endured cardiac condition was aggravated by infected tonsils. She was going to take him on a sea voyage to Europe, where a tonsillectomy would be performed, before he returned to work.

With that, Louis B. Mayer took charge. In three years in the story department, I had seen little of the studio's big boss, and then mostly at larger gatherings or the picnics and holiday parties he attended. He was conspicuously absent from the big Christmas party.

As I came to know him better I realized he adhered to a code of principles that he rigidly observed. He was masterful at the art of keeping the morale of his employees high. He knew the Christmas party blew away alcoholic and sexual restraints and while he didn't approve, his absence was designed to let the men and women of the work force celebrate the high accomplishments of their dream factory.

The need for Mayer to pick up the reins that had fallen from Thalberg's hands was opportune for him. His friendship and support of President Herbert Hoover through the late 1920s had won him an invitation to be that chief executive's first overnight guest at the White House, which he accepted. It also brought him an offer from Hoover to be American Ambassador to Turkey, which he rejected. Hoover was defeated for a second term in November 1932. As a result, Mayer was considering spending more time movie-making when Thalberg's sudden collapse made it imperative that he do so at once. The country's impending change from a Republican to a Democrat regime was timely, too, for him, ending his political aspirations.

Unlike Thalberg, Mayer knew few writers and less about current story material. He had a few favorite books, long outdated, recalled from childhood. He often reminded Corbaley and me how he would enjoy seeing them on film, but never insisted on it and didn't object to our indifference. Knowing his power, this attitude increased my admiration for him.

The swearing-in of the newly-elected President was moved up from its traditional date in March to January 1, 1933. Then, the first card played by Franklin Roosevelt's New Deal was to close all the banks, declaring a moratorium on all monetary transactions to give the unsettled nation time to assess its accounts. It also gave studio writers who were inclined to live ahead of their means a once-in-a-lifetime opportunity.

"I love it," said Hoppy. "It allows every fucking deadbeat to put the bite on Louis B. Mayer, who's got more money than the banks, anyway."

Actor-writer-director Gregory Ratoff, who mixed his Russian accent with fractured English, was indignant. "That writer-fellow Gene Markey is a crook," he fumed. "I gave him a check on a bank where I have no money and he cashed it!"

The bank closings highlighted the darkness overwhelming those first weeks of 1933, and film company bosses were quick to take advantage. They called on all workers to cut their salaries in half for the duration of the crisis.

At MGM, a number of contract writers were asked to the largest projection room on the lot, along with some actors, directors and department heads. Quiet and subdued, the group waited in the dim light for the star to make his entrance.

After a suitable period of time, Mayer walked in slowly and faced his audience. His eyes were red, his expression grief-stricken and he had an unusual stubble of beard on his chin. He spread his hands in a supplicating gesture and said "My friends. . . ." It was a poignant moment. He was bereft of words.

Lionel Barrymore was one of the studio's first directors when talk came in. He had become a treasured character actor befitting his heritage as a member of one of the theatre's royal families. He had a husky and unmistakable voice.

"Don't worry, L. B.," he called out. "We all know why we're here. We're with you."

But Hungarian playwright Ernest Vajda rose to his feet and protested, because the company's income was high, as was its profit.

"So, there is no reason to cut our pay," he declared.

Mayer, surprised, had no dialogue in reply but Barrymore did.

"Mr. Vajda is like a man on his way to the guillotine wanting to stop for a manicure." That line brought down the house.

Actress May Robson picked up her cue. "As the oldest person in the room, Mr. Mayer, I will take the cut."

Child actor Freddie Bartholomew shouted, "As the young-est person in the room, Mr. Mayer, I will take the cut."

Mayer beamed, his voice restored. "No more than eight weeks. I, Louis B. Mayer, will work to see that you get back every penny when this terrible emergency is over."

The cut was voted.

Mayer and Ben Thau were a few footsteps behind me as we crossed an iron bridge to the executive office building and I heard Mayer ask the talent expert, "How did I do?" I didn't hear Thau's answer, but have no doubt any judge of acting would have given Mayer the highest possible rating for his artistry.

MGM restored full salaries in six weeks. None was ever returned, but the cuts went deeper than paychecks, for in a short time the blood they drew would bring about the formation of protective guilds for all participants in the creative arts of the film world.

Meanwhile, the unsettled manpower was further shaken up, but by the hands of nature.

My friendship with Richard Rodgers began when we were twelve and sent to a boys camp by our parents so they could enjoy their summers. Our association continued during winters at Broadway matinees of musical shows by Jerome Kern. Dick Rodgers always knew he would be a composer and I recall a conversation we had in a camp canoe when he mourned that he would need more than one lifetime to develop all the melodies churning in his head. He practiced piano in the camp lodge for four hours every day while others like myself dawdled away our time at sports in which we were highly incompetent.

Rodgers had composed the scores of ten Broadway musical comedies when our paths came together again at MGM. Late on the afternoon of March 11, 1933, he called from the music department where he worked with lyricist Lorenz Hart. They had just finished the words and music to a new song and asked if I'd like to hear it.

I hurried over. Hart was an adorable dwarf-like fellow, prepared to demonstrate the new lyric in a voice he described as "low but disagreeable." It was the title song of a new film *I Married An Angel.*

Dick played on a broken-down upright as Hart sang, "Have you heard, I married an angel. . . ?" when a low rumble from beneath us provided an unexpected accompaniment.

"What's that?" Dick asked and stopped playing.

Nature answered him. The lights went out, the room shook violently and the piano moved away from the three of us and rammed a far wall. It was scary. The room was down a long dark corridor in a dilapidated wooden building. Escape along that route seemed an adventure none of us were anxious to pursue.

A second shake moved the piano near a window that was high and small and nailed closed to prevent break-ins from the outside. Nailing it closed also served to prevent us from getting out, a move we considered very desirable at that moment.

Rodgers was equal to the occasion. He grabbed the piano stool and threw it through the glass. Then he leaped onto the piano and dived out into the street. Hart followed, but his diminutive height made it difficult to climb up on the piano. When he succeeded, he, too, leaped after his partner.

They were gone in a matter of seconds. Here I was, with two friends playing and singing and suddenly jumping out of a window. It seemed an extremely comic scene.

At that instant, a tremendous crash shook the building. The whole structure seemed to be coming down (I found out later the brick chimney had toppled); it was no time to hang around for a laugh. I, too, scrambled up on the piano and jumped, tumbling onto an auto road strewn with broken glass.

I was in the path of a motorist who braked abruptly. He asked, "What the hell is going on?" He had seen a piano stool and three men come flying through a window. Larry Hart announced that we had made a profound scientific discovery. "Earthquakes aren't felt in moving cars!" he solemnly declared.

Earthquake Syndrome was endemic to Southern Californians. No matter how strong the latest shock, someone always said, "You ain't seen nothin' yet," and guaranteed the place would be leveled by the coming Big One.

The quake we survived convinced Marie and me to live closer to *terra firma* than a fourth-floor apartment. We moved out of the building Upton Sinclair called "Platinum Blonde" and into a Beverly Hills house with a tennis court. Marie and I had irrevocably turned our back on the injunction "Never buy anything you can't put on The Chief!"

The man who sold us our new home was its builder, who had felt the pinch of the depression. More than the house, he was especially proud of the tennis court. It looked just fine, constructed of concrete with painted white lines, a wire fence around it and a net in the middle, all the requisites for a court to be proud of.

We invited some tennis-playing friends over for our first weekend, but as the games went on, they had trouble keeping balls in the court. It resulted in a lot of arguments over what was in or out until examination revealed that the builder knew what a court looked like but didn't think it needed any particular measurements. He had designed it catch-as-catch-can. Play stopped for six weeks while we had it rebuilt into regulation size.

In this period of change, something similar happened to our piano, acquired for peanuts at a house sale down the street. I was satisfied with it until Richard Rodgers came to visit. Everyone who plays piano loves to try each new one they see, like golfers viewing a new golf course. Of our piano, Rodgers didn't express an opinion, he just sat down and stared at it for a moment, then with a look of cold contempt, got up and walked away. Out of humiliation came education. Marie and I went out and bought a Steinway.

Our ability to indulge in extravagant practices in the heart of a great depression was due to the comfortable way of life in a great film studio. In three years, my daily relationship with writers had settled into an amusing and pleasant occupation, searching for and sometimes finding a great story idea was exciting. The supervision of the reading, stenographic and research departments was easy, thanks to the women running them. At holiday soirees and picnics, Louis B. Mayer periodically indulged in emotional speeches, promising everyone "as long as you do your job here you have one for life." Incredible as it may seem in later years, I continued in this notoriously insecure profession without asking for or needing a contract. That I did so speaks volumes for the honesty and methods of Mayer's operation. In contrast, just a few years ahead lay a stint with Samuel Goldwyn, who had voiced as one of his principles: "A verbal contract isn't worth the paper it's written on."

Mayer was a brilliant individual and an unparalleled administrator. He adhered to his often-voiced precept: "I hire people for their brains and I'm not such a fool that I don't let them use them." Writer Leonard Spiegelgass said, "He invented the movie industry!"

His brusque exterior and innate toughness were melted by sob stories. Carey Wilson was hit by the costs of a divorce that wiped out his finances. He made an appeal to Mayer and said that when he saw Mayer's eyes glisten with tears, he knew he'd get what he needed.

Mayer also brought to this turn in his career an instinctive sense of showmanship, a talent for discovering stars and enormous changes in the production system. However, there were several dimensions to filmmaking he didn't know. No longer could the supervisors turn to Thalberg to correct a flawed scenario or suggest retakes that recharged a film that missed fire. Some learned this the hard way.

In the early days of sound, revue-type musical films proved popular and Harry Rapf was looked on as the specialist at that form. His *March of Time* floundered in production and the incomplete project languished on the shelf.

Before taking ill, Thalberg approved a new start for it. The filmed elements were pulled from the vaults and the company's publicity head, Howard Dietz, who wrote lyrics and stage revues on the side, came from New York to head up a veritable army of writers. They wrote introductions for stars as well as new skits and numbers. While waiting for the players to be available, comedians Jimmy Durante, Ted Healy and Jack Pearl, all from Broadway's nightclubs, filmed the introductions.

Rodgers and Hart wrote new songs; the comedians announced that Jean Harlow was to sing and the stars they were about to see were Joan Crawford, Marie Dressler, and Clark Gable. But before these luminaries stepped before a camera,

Mayer commanded Rapf to sneak-preview the footage that was ready, with a new title, *Hollywood Party.*

Late one afternoon executives, department heads and production personnel boarded a big red trolley car, especially outfitted, at a spur that ran directly into the studio. While the car lumbered through the Pacific Electric tracks into the inner city and then out through fragrant orange groves toward San Bernardino, those on board enjoyed a sumptuous buffet dinner and played cards.

That run took about two and a half hours. After a quick visit to the dinner buffet, Mayer and Rapf sat down to bridge. The stakes were low but tensions were high.

Mayer was only an occasional bridge player but Rapf was persistent at it, even though his skills were questionable. He once played in a game where, when the bidding was done, the players got into a long conversation. When they resumed their game, a wrong player led a card and the successful bidders absently took the defensive. After the last card was played they realized their error and, unable to figure how to score it, called an authority at a prestigious bridge club.

"What do we do now?" Rapf asked.

"Stop playing bridge," was the instant reply.

On the preview night of *Hollywood Party,* Rapf was worried by the impending display of an unready and, to say the least, unconventional public showing. His last-minute plea to Mayer to abort it was refused. Mayer saw no reason to do so. Unlike the sneak preview of *Lullaby* with only the producer, director, writer and myself in attendance, Mayer wanted a full complement of studio employees.

Test director Felix Feist, Jr., the son of the company's sales head, was Mayer's partner. Both were dealt hands with high cards and equally high possibilities.

Mayer opened his bid with two spades, his partner topped it with four no-trump. Visual signals were a no-no but Mayer's frown revealed his thoughts. He expected to seal off the bidding with a loud "Five spades," enabling him to play the cards, but Feist closed him out with a try for seven no-trump, a grand slam that gave him the playing hand. He went down five points. Mayer stalked off to the far end of the car and rode the rest of the way in a stony rage.

If that wasn't enough to indicate the stars weren't out for *Hollywood Party* that night, the preview without stars was the final blow. A confused audience hooted loudly and the theatre manager stridently accused the executives of screening disconnected film clips at his expense.

It was obvious that Rapf's attempt to jettison the preview was a valid one. Mayer called the movie a hodgepodge. He would not sanction further filming and no stars would be made available for it. "Just release it the way it is," he said.

Averting his eyes from even the most sympathetic associates on board, Rapf sat in the rear of the car as it lumbered bumpily back to the studio, and wept.

The story treadmill continued nonstop and, returning from a scouting trip to northern California with a suitcase of manuscripts to be read, I found a message from Bernie Hyman to see him urgently.

He asked that I fire a writer he hired during my absence.

"What's wrong with him?" I asked.

"He's the wrong Smith," said the producer.

During my absence Hyman asked Frank Capra to suggest a writer and the director recommended a man named Smith. When Hyman set out to find Smith he couldn't recall his given name. He told my secretary he thought it started with "W". My secretary told Hyman that a writer named Walton Hall Smith was available. It sounded like the recommended name and he was brought in and given the assignment.

Several days later the producer saw Capra again and discovered that he meant a Smith named *Wallace*. Walton Hall Smith's material was scrapped unread.

Had it been a Capra movie plot, the wrong Smith would develop into a world-beater. But it didn't work that way. Wallace Smith became a noted screenwriter. Walton Hall Smith faded from the literary scene. Frank Capra made more films about Smiths, but none about a Mr. Smith Going to Hollywood.

The creative imagination of Charley Lederer evoked delight in all the studio executives. That irrepressible joker was the court jester, bouncing on to the writer's payroll when he needed money and off it when he felt an urge to travel. The supervisors often sent for him because he had an ability to invent instant situations, as when Hyman posed a story problem to him and asked him how he would meet it.

"This boy's sitting next to this girl in this train," explained the producer. "Let's say you're the boy and the girl ignores you. What do you do?"

"I burn my hat," said Charley.

"What does that mean?"

"Well, I put my straw hat on my lap while I light my cigarette and don't notice that I've set my hat on fire. I look out the window and let her look at the burning hat. She lets out a scream . . . so, take it from there."

His abilities more than offset the stigma of nepotism attached to his relationship to "Aunt Marion" Davies.

Nepotism begins at home, sneered funny man "Hoppy" when it was announced that David Oliver Selznick would be joining the company as a top-ranking producer. Married to Louis B. Mayer's daughter Irene, Selznick's pending arrival elicited a derisive "The Son-in-law Also Rises" and scorn swept the studio.

Selznick knew immediately that he was in for a rough time. The studio belonged to Thalberg, the loyalties of the personnel were entirely with their stricken leader.

He engaged in serious soul-searching when Mayer first broached the idea that he join the studio staff. He also called Thalberg in Europe for approval, receiving a whole-hearted go-ahead. He told Thalberg that he believed personal publicity a requisite part of movie-making and intended to take screen credit as the producer of his films.

Thalberg offered no objections, but said he would adhere

to his own view that "Credit you give yourself isn't worth having." He sent word to his associates that they were free to identify their films as producer and advocated that they do so, rather than let Selznick's be the only production executive name on MGM pictures. To a man, they added their names to the screen credits. Thalberg never did.

During his New York stopover on the way to Europe, Thalberg made a new deal with company president Nicholas M. Schenck, agreeing to give up full supervision of all productions. On his return, he was to concentrate on making his own films.

It wasn't what he wanted; he preferred to carry on total responsibilities because of his conviction that he only had a short time to live and the hours he worked would not affect it. But he acceded to the change of career in accordance with the pleading of his wife, the wish of his physician, and the desires of Mayer and Schenck.

Mayer had long feared that Thalberg's chronic cardiac condition might suddenly terminate the studio head's life. But after the new collapse, Mayer sought to find a back-up executive. His first choice was David Selznick, who had previously experienced running a studio operation under B. P. Schulberg at Paramount and later with Howard Hughes at RKO, but he preferred to be an independent producer. He began what would be a long search, in the course of which he tapped such varied talents as Director Howard Hawks and Producer Walter Wanger, both under contract to MGM at the time, but none measured up to Thalberg's talents or remained long in the job. In his disillusionment, Mayer took over the reins himself. Actually he was ably fitted to it from his own pioneer producing days.

Thalberg's approval of Selznick's joining the staff at MGM on equal terms as producer opened the way for him to enter into the big Culver City plant. His position, while important, was much less so than chief of operations and dulled the stings of nepotism, which he felt very keenly. He was an independent in the full meaning of the word, a resourceful creator, resolute, dynamic and ambitious. He intended to show these characteristics to all who heaped scorn on him because of his relationship to Mayer.

Charley Lederer was unconcerned by his own relationship to a prominent star. He sauntered into the outer office of Selznick's suite, motivated as usual by a love of mischief.

Dinner At Eight was to be Selznick's first MGM production. The play, by George S. Kaufman and Edna Ferber, interwove the lives of characters very much in the style of *Grand Hotel* and, like that film, was to be enacted by a truly all-star cast. A serious omission amongst them drew Lederer to visit Selznick.

Told that the producer was not in, Lederer informed the secretary he was bothered because Greta Garbo wouldn't appear in *Dinner At Eight*. He felt that Selznick's marriage to Louis B. Mayer's daughter qualified him to obtain the great Swedish actress. Pleased by the incredulous look on the secretary's face, he embroidered his theme. One reason for her look was that Selznick had come into the outer office behind Lederer and was hearing him suggest that the producer should have married Mayer's two daughters in order to procure Garbo. Charley was having a wonderful time, a monologue he intended to repeat in word for word detail the next time he saw Ben Hecht.

Meanwhile, Selznick backed silently out and crossed the corridor to summon Eddie Mannix. Calling upon some of the expertise he acquired in his earlier career as a bouncer at Palisades Amusement Park, Mannix grabbed the prankster by the scruff of the neck and, with true professional polish, propelled him outside the studio gate. Lederer was complaining loudly that Mannix had lost his sense of humor but the studio manager ordered the guards never to let him come through the portals again.

Certain he could explain it was just a harmless joke, Lederer moved down the street and flagged art director Cedric Gibbons, who was driving in. Gibbons hid him in the trunk of his car, then let him out near Mannix's office. Again, Lederer was summarily escorted out the gate.

My instruction to take him off the payroll was in the nature of another joke, for Mannix and Selznick and I knew Charley would be on it again sooner or later. Producers loved having him around. I did, too, especially when he arranged for Marie and me to weekend at the Hearst Ranch at San Simeon, the most dearly desired invitation in all California. In the meantime, Charley went East to houseguest with Ben Hecht and when he got there, he telegraphed Mannix, ARRIVED SAFE. LOVE.

Chapter Nine

Very much like Charley Lederer, his aunt Marion Davies was known to her coworkers as a generous, delightful person with a sharp sense of humor. She also handled the immense persona of William Randolph Hearst with tact and charm.

He was always "The Chief" to her, as her boss, her lover and probably because the mastheads of his newspapers always listed him as Editor-in-Chief. Their production headquarters inside the studio compound was a luxurious bungalow that Hearst owned, complete with living quarters.

Soon after Franklin D. Roosevelt became President, even before he announced his cabinet, I met with Hearst and Davies in the bungalow to discuss stories for her future films. The talk turned to casting her next picture when we were interrupted by a phone call from the White House. In somewhat awed silence, I heard him say, "Well, Frank, he'll be okay but I think you can do better," followed by, "Personally, I'd favor him more for Agriculture than Navy." At this point, Marion whispered, "The Chief is casting, too."

She was no stranger to wealth and power when she met Hearst. Christened Marion Douras, she was the daughter of a New York City magistrate who, within the limits of a civic courtroom, wielded influence and political muscle.

Show business attracted her, as it did her sister Rose, Charley's mother, who married a Broadway theatrical producer. The young Marion, blonde and beautiful, danced in revues and musical comedies in the 1920s.

Often, on evenings at home, I put aside the reading Kate Corbaley demanded I devour and wrote my impressions of the lively characters passing in parade around me. Among them, was the following:

"WR's massive efforts to promote Marion Davies as a superior goddess obscures her true values. She has a distinct flair, talent and style and reveals onscreen a hoydenish slapstick comedienne with an infectious grin, as appealing as Mabel Normand, the only one I find worthy of comparison. It's too bad this big man's over-sell causes the public to distrust what he says. It is no back street or back page romance, the public knows the score. Every picture she makes is sickeningly praised in his papers which irritates rather than stimulates his readers."

Hearst may well have excused his actions on grounds that love is blind, for the affection they shared did have a kind of imperishable quality to it, although few writers described their idyll as a love affair. It was, moreover, complicated by a wife, ever present if not ever visible. Millicent Hearst accepted the inevitable; she remained in New York, quietly holding him to his marriage vows. Their four sons maintained a precarious allegiance to both parents and accepted Marion, too. That situation was part of the mud splattered on Hearst by his enemies, of whom he had multitudes. He and his love stayed aloof from the dirt heaped on them. When Hearst's own reporters mentioned him in publicity stories about Marion, he was identified as "her great and good friend." This, at least, was no overstatement.

Discussing his aunt with Charley Lederer, I expressed curiosity at her meeting with Hearst. This, he said, is how it happened.

All the dancing girls in a Broadway musical comedy were invited to an after-theatre party by Philadelphia millionaire James P. Widener, who was enamored of Marion's best friend, Julanne Johnston. Under their dinner plates at this midnight soiree, every girl discovered a crisp new hundred-dollar bill. All but Julanne—she found a certified check for twenty-five thousand dollars!

"I'm going to buy everything I ever wanted," she said to Marion. They arranged to meet in the lobby of the Astor Hotel next morning.

"Julie dashed from store to store," said Lederer. "She bought fur coats, jewelry, and an automobile. By late afternoon, she spent the whole twenty-five thousand. Then, completely spent themselves, they were back at the Astor. Julie thanked Marion for her company and left her there."

"All day," said Lederer, "Marion thought somewhere on this shopping expedition Julie would invite her to buy a dress or a piece of jewelry. But that never happened."

"Now, the excitement over, a tired Marion was struck by the full shock of disappointment. She settled into a chair in the hotel lobby and hid her eyes while she held back tears. Then she felt something pressed into her palm. It was a thousand dollar bill. Standing in front of her was William Randolph Hearst."

"I saw your tears," he explained. "Maybe this will chase them away."

"And that was how it started," said Lederer. I repeated the story to Marie.

"There you go again," she said. "Believing the unbelievable."

She was sure Hearst knew Marion's identity, if indeed he saw her at the Astor Hotel in tears. And she knew for a fact that Marion's face and legs had constantly adorned his Sunday supplements. "I bet he was after her all the time."

She indicated an advance copy of a London play, *The Barretts of Wimpole Street,* that I had brought home. She had read it in one sitting.

"If you're looking for a true love story," she said, "get them to make that one."

I told her Kate Corbaley had outlined it to Thalberg before the Christmas party and he turned it down.

"Mr. Mayer's in charge now. Take it up with him."

I gave her a look. As a loyal Thalberg adherent, I wasn't out to prove him wrong. But although Mayer never professed to match Thalberg's judgments on story possibilities, he was quite aware of the need to keep ahead of the studio's huge program. And the very next day, he summoned Kate and me to a projection room to see a German film with him.

It was a period piece called *Maskerade,* a schmaltzy concoction of froth and charm that Kate and Mayer found totally charming while I succumbed to the attractions of its petite, sloe-eyed leading lady. Its presentation to the studio as a possible remake was a tribute to the manner with which Mayer injected familial pride and loyalty into his staff. It had been sent over by director Clarence Brown, not as a film he wished to make, but simply one that entertained him while on a European vacation and one that Mayer might find worthy of fashioning over in America.

This impromptu story meeting concluded with Mayer deciding to contact Brown in Europe to purchase the rights. Walking out of the projection room I mentioned rather casually that I found the girl in the film very interesting. Less than a month after this, the studio boss called me to his office to meet Luise Rainer, introducing me to the small, intense actress as the one who recommended she be brought to California. With her luminous dark eyes fixed on me, a grateful smile on her lips, it was a most ideal way to start a friendship.

Her style and mannerisms reminded me of a reigning German film star, Elisabeth Bergner, but our friendship took a less endearing turn when I mentioned the resemblance to her. She asked, "Who's she?" and walked away in a fury when I refused to take her question seriously.

But she wasn't angry long. She decided I was her only friend in Hollywood, as plans to adapt *Maskerade,* now called *Escapade,* moved so swiftly that hardly any time elapsed before it was ready for production. Then tragedy struck full force. Luise wouldn't be in it.

A concensus of production brains decided her English needed improvement and anyway, the story fitted costars Myrna Loy and William Powell. Miss Rainer was assigned a schedule of lessons with voice and acting coaches. She fell onto the window seat in my office in tears, her life and career suspended in an endless time lag.

My office became headquarters for her to while away the hours between her hated lessons. A daily occupant on the window seat, she mourned the loss of the role that brought her to the United States, completely destroying my working routine while wishing I would hurry films that she could make in the future. She had a special desire to star in a story she outlined to me, portraying a girl who went to the airport in Rome to await a lover flying to her from Africa in his own plane. But instead of a glorious reunion, airport officials broke the news to her he had crashed and was killed. It was autobiographical, she said, and not only would she write it but, to prove there had been such a relationship, she came to the office one day wearing a kind of crazy-quilt dress, made, she said, from the cover of the couch on which she and the dead flier had made wild and passionate love.

She also took a friendly interest in my personal well-being and, learning that Marie was out of town, invited me to dinner at her Malibu beach house. "I will fix our meal with my own two hands." It was hardly the kind of invitation a lonely husband turns down and I showed up hungrily at sundown.

She was having a loud, yelling telephone conversation with her mother in Germany when I arrived. Suddenly she was cut off, whereupon she notified a phone company executive she wouldn't pay for the call. That made for a heated dispute that lasted nearly an hour.

Then, however, peace reigned. She relaxed at the piano and played *Liebestraum* quite beautifully. I was impressed. I was also impressed when we went out on the beach and she identified all the stars and constellations shining down on us.

It was her dinner that I found less impressive. She had indeed fixed it with her own two hands, a turgid slab of cold calf liver, an out-take from her lunch. She shoved it between two huge slices of bread. This gruesome offering marked a turning point in my life; I was never again able to eat calf liver.

Marie believed strongly in social reciprocation and on her

return invited Luise to our next party. The German actress was a lovely, decorative guest, sitting pensively on a parlor couch most of the evening, rising only to play *Liebestraum* on the piano to loud applause. But she refused to do an encore. Neither would she step outside and identify the constellations.

She was lounging in her usual spot on my office window seat when an urgent message came for her to come at once to the stage where *Escapade* was shooting. She darted away as if she sensed her moment of destiny had arrived, as indeed it had. Myrna Loy had walked out of the film in a salary row. Luise stepped into the part she played in the original production.

She never returned to my office and we never dined again. In time I was to introduce her to Clifford Odets, the New York playwright with whom she would share a brief, unhappy marriage. But that introduction was three years ahead, although still encompassed in the gaudy life of the Thirties.

The mystery why she only played *Liebestraum* and wouldn't identify the stars twice was solved by Odets, normally a decent, sympathetic fellow but who came to strongly dislike the girl he was once so eager to wed. He labeled them sidelight pieces, neon signs she used to show off extra abilities in addition to her acting talents. He claimed she could only play that one piano piece and could only recognize the positions of the stars during a single week of the year.

While I might fault her attempts at cooking, there was none to be found with her brief career in Hollywood. Before she returned to Europe, Luise won two Academy Oscars. To do so, she successfully lost the Teutonic accent that so nearly cost her the lead in *Escapade.* Her first Award was for playing a famous French beauty, Anna Held, in *The Great Ziegfeld,* and her second Oscar would be for the Chinese peasant she portrayed in Pearl Buck's *The Good Earth* when Irving Thalberg was back in stride as an independent producer.

Charley Lederer and Irving Thalberg returned to the studio the same day in September 1933, but not together. Thalberg was driven through the auto gate in his wife's Rolls Royce, a huge white monstrosity. Jim, their chauffeur, doubled as bodyguard; he had to use his muscular ability to ward off the producer's admirers. Thalberg's welcome was so joyous it could have sent him back to his doctor.

Thalberg's appearance was celebrated at a luncheon in the executive bungalow. In a short speech he assured his associates he was in good health, largely because of the surgical work on his tonsils, which, although a minor operation, had encountered major difficulties.

"The best doctor in Germany refused to do it because of the rise of the Nazi party and its leader, Adolf Hitler. They are hell-bent on exterminating the Jewish race." The doctor worried, Thalberg said, that if the tonsil operation went wrong, people would say he deliberately caused the death of a prominent Jewish-American film producer. "I tried to laugh him out of it," he went on, "and told him the risk I was taking was larger than his, but fellows, what's happening in Germany today is no laughing matter. I was awakened every morning by brown-shirted Nazis marching outside my hotel window, their boots thundering on the pavement. They shouted at the top of their voices, 'Germany today and tomorrow the world.' It wasn't the most pleasant way to open your eyes!"

Charley Lederer strolled in that day in autumn, arm in arm with Charlie MacArthur (who was writing a script for Thalberg) and Ben Hecht (who was doing the same for Selznick). The trio was greeted by Eddie Mannix who must have forgotten he had permanently banished Lederer from the lot. He readily agreed to find an office for Hecht's "assistant hack," as he termed his friend.

Thalberg made his need for important stories his first priority, and Kate and I began daily meetings to recommend material. Almost immediately, he had a surprise for us. After seeing Katharine Cornell, an actress he greatly admired, in *The Barretts of Wimpole Street* on Broadway, he had changed his mind and now he wished to make the play into a film with Norma Shearer. But we had a surprise for him. Marion Davies had also seen it and purchased the screen rights. He shook his head dismally and said, "They'll laugh her off the screen."

Reflecting on the contents of the plot, he zeroed in on why he thought Hearst bought it. "He has this hang-up about seeing her wear pants. It's a sexual thing, a fixation."

The scene in *The Barretts of Wimpole Street* that Thalberg was certain had roused Hearst's interest was when the invalid Elizabeth Browning wore pants as poet Robert Browning carried her away from her father's home. That reminded Kate of an alternate yarn.

In our story file, with possibilities for Norma Shearer, was a Civil War spy comedy, *Operator 13,* with a plot that called for her to be dressed as a man through the entire film. It was by Robert W. Chambers, whose popular romances constantly appeared in Hearst's *Cosmopolitan Magazine.* "WR will buy it in a minute," said Thalberg. "But if I suggest we swap it for *The Barretts* he'll get his back up. He's always been jealous of Norma's success."

He knew I was making my long-delayed trek to the Hearst Ranch and intended to go that weekend. "How about you?" he asked. "Don't mention Norma, just point out that *Operator 13* will appeal to Marion's fans more than a starchy character like Elizabeth Browning. Be discreet but see what you can do and, of course, drop in the fact she'll be masquerading in a man's uniform."

I promised to do my best, although what was to be a weekend holiday had now turned into a business mission.

Early Friday morning, Marie and I started up the coast road toward San Simeon in our small roadster, as convertible cars were called. The top was folded back. The rumble seat, an automotive term also fated for oblivion in our changing language, held our luggage.

Ever since we arrived in Hollywood, Marie and I had heard about the parties at the Hearst Ranch. Of all the gaudy soirees in the movie colony, these were the ultimate, the most highly desired. By all reports, they had an aura of glamour shining through even the worst of them, for example, the one that honored P. G. Wodehouse was described to me by his wife and daughter as "absolutely ghastly."

The party was a Hawaiian style luau, for which Hearst imported grass skirts and leis direct from the islands. Native musicians and tropical decorations and sand underfoot transformed the great castle into an authentic setting for the occasion. All the guests were told that costume was *de rigeur,* and, incidentally, they were expected to be barefoot.

What made it "ghastly" for Mrs. Wodehouse and daughter Leonora was that shy, retiring "Plummy" had no intention of joining in the fun. "I wouldn't put on a grass skirt for W. R. Hearst or anyone else in the whole wide world," he told them.

The Wodehouse women proceeded downstairs and were confronted by their host, a towering spectacle in his shaggy yellow raiment of the tropics. Where, he asked, was the eminent author? The Wodehouse women were no longer mortified by their man's antisocial behavior. They had grown resigned and even defended his opposition to costume parties. Annoyed, Hearst directed them to return upstairs and inform the author this one would be his initiation to the custom. Mr. Hearst commanded it!

Late in the party, the errant guest made his appearance, but he was wearing no grassy habiliment as he faced his host. For an instant, both behemoths stood smiling at each other. Then Hearst spoke gently and dangerously.

"I sent word I want all my guests to be in costume."

The author indicated his tuxedo.

"I am in costume, sir. I'm an Englishman in the tropics and we always dress for dinner!"

He pushed past his speechless host and joined his wife and daughter.

During our day-long drive to San Simeon, I recalled for Marie another tale of the Hearst Ranch. Its hero was writer Gene Markey, a lover of gorgeous women usually in the act of marrying or divorcing some beauteous film star and, incidental to such activities, a great raconteur and quite good screen writer. A regular guest at the Ranch, he arrived one day during a heavy rainstorm and was sitting before the fireplace in the great hall, reading. His preoccupation with the book in hand caused him to ignore recognizable redheaded Lili Damita, a lady he had never met, who had been horseback riding and was standing between him and the fireplace, intent on drying her tweedy riding outfit. The blazing logs, he estimated, were the size of a normal freight car, befitting the hugeness of everything in Hearst's domain. To hasten the drying process, Miss Damita moved nearer to the flames and when they licked too close, stepped away. Those movements finally distracted Markey. He looked up and after watching her for a moment said, "If that's for me, please, not too well done."

At sunset, *La Cuesta Encantada* was ahead and high above us, gleaming magically as we pulled alongside a guard at the base of the hill.

Finding our names on his list of acceptable intruders, he instructed us to stay in the car while climbing the twisting five miles ahead. Ropes dangled from tall poles at various intervals, a pull on them lifted gates that allowed us to go past exotic animals that looked ferocious but merely eyed us in a disinterested way. Near the top, lions and tigers roared from zoo-like cages.

Weather-beaten packing cases were strewn on the lawn some fifty yards from the castle steps. Inside them were parts of an ancient castle the publisher purchased in Europe and shipped to California but hadn't yet got around to opening. It was reported they had lain there ten years, adding to their claim to antiquity.

We passed a 105-foot swimming pool, fed by a cascade of rippling water. This outdoor pool merged into an equally large one indoors; Venetian gondolas were floating among pillars that supported part of the building overhead. The indoor pool was all gold and lapis lazuli mosiacs. No one used either pool during our stay.

We were met at the steps of the castle by a galaxy of servants who whisked our car away with the luggage still in it. Hearst and Marion greeted us in the great hall and when we reached our room (which was once part of a chateau in France, even to the doorknobs), our clothes were freshly pressed and neatly hung in closets or placed in bureau drawers.

Our room was in the castle proper, La Casa Grande. Three guest houses were nearby. There were fifty-eight bedrooms and forty-nine bathrooms on the hill but on this weekend there were only twenty-seven guests. Hearst and Marion were apologetic that we chose such a quiet time. There would be a sedate Sunday picnic; I had hoped to enjoy some exotic carousing but there wouldn't even be a grass skirt to wear.

The guests included three Hearst executives. Under the Chief's system of ownership, each of his periodicals was an entity presided over by an individual designated as publisher. It was an imposing title but in name only for, as I saw then, they all took their orders from Hearst. A little way down the hill was a shack in which telegraph machines crackled with commands and personally written editorials from the big boss. I could easily visualize puppets of the great paper empire snapping to attention in time belts around the globe as each dispatch arrived.

Marion asked us to come down at six. As dutiful guests, we showed up precisely at that time. Hearst disapproved of drinking, although he certainly knew that many of his guests looked on the cocktail hour as the most important in the day.

The situation was neatly resolved. Liquor was served until nearly seven-thirty. Then, an increasing nervousness pervaded our hostess. Her eyes watched for the glow of the red light in a wall that indicated the publisher's private elevator was descending from his personal quarters. She signaled the servants, who sprang into action. It was a slow elevator, which wasn't surprising, as it had once been a confessional box in an ancient church. When Hearst stepped out, he was greeted by his warmed-up guests without a drink in sight.

On the Friday and Saturday nights we were there, a Marion Davies film was shown in the projection room. In both films, which I had already seen, I noted that Marion wore pants. After each show Hearst whipped up Welsh rarebits on equipment wheeled into the projection room. He took great delight in doing the cooking and serving. And despite his prejudices, he urged all rarebit eaters to partake of beer. "Rarebits without beer aren't rarebits," he advised, like a good editorial writer.

He also permitted wine at dinner. But wine wasn't needed to intoxicate the imagination about the magnificence of life at the Ranch. The huge, long refectory or dining hall was spectacular. Banners bearing ancient coats-of-arms crossed and crisscrossed each other high overhead. Huge tapestries depicting ancient armies in action draped the walls. The fireplace sizzled with burning logs that were tree-trunk wide; ordinary branches would have seemed like toothpicks.

The dining table was half unused, its full size dwarfing the group. Hearst and Marion sat across from each other, midway. Stretching lengthwise from them were their guests. New arrivals were seated nearest to them. As others arrived, one found his or her place card moved down the table. At the furthest end of the assembled diners sat a couple who had been at the Ranch so long they, themselves, had forgotten the date of their arrival. Besides the three newspaper executives, the party was made up of a smattering of movie people and one of Hearst's sons, George, who was quiet, subdued, worried and grossly overweight, all of which he plainly showed.

There had been discussion of a Sunday picnic at an often-used glade on the Ranch, which covered 245,000 acres. Marion thought it would be more exciting for us to picnic at a smaller castle fifty miles away, where we would all stay overnight. It met with mixed reactions, especially from the three publishers eager to leave for home Sunday night. Marion pictured an evening at the distant ranchhouse as brimming with fun and no business appointment was so important it couldn't be delayed twenty-four hours. Even when Hearst pointed out to her that there weren't twenty-nine beds in the other castle, she smilingly downplayed that problem by suggesting his DC-3 plane could fly enough cots from San Francisco. However, Marion's desire was vetoed by the Chief who preferred a common, everyday type picnic to occupy our Sunday just three miles away.

It was a common, everyday picnic, but only in a manner of speaking. Guests who chose to reach the picnic grounds by horseback were driven in chauffeured limousines to a point where horses were tethered, about two miles from the site. After they rode in, grooms returned the horses to the stable.

Waiting at the picnic grounds was the entire servant corps of the Ranch, complete with mobile stoves and refrigerators. The food was exactly as if it might have been served in the dining hall. After the meal, all the picnickers were taken back to the castle by car.

That afternoon, I had a story session with Hearst and Marion about their future films. Without downplaying *The Barretts of Wimpole Street* too strongly, I stressed my preference for lighter stories for her, such as the comic antics available as a spy fighting the Civil War in the garb of a trousered soldier if she did *Operator 13*.

Hearst was interested, and said he would think about it. When I reported this, Thalberg also enlisted the help of Louis B. Mayer who promised to secure Gary Cooper to costar. In the end, the conspiracy worked and Hearst traded off a movie with a single trouser episode for one that allowed Marion to wear them all the way to the closing sequence.

Among the newspaper men at the ranch that weekend was A. J. Kobler, the publisher of New York's *Daily Mirror,* and during the picnic he heard we were driving to Los Angeles that evening. He wanted to go along. The forecast was for cold and blustery weather and I warned him it would be an uncomfortable ride in the unprotected rumble seat. But he wanted to go with us.

Each day there I had seen the quiet trio of publishers waiting in the great hall for a summons to the upper regions and they always entered the elevator looking apprehensive and distraught, to descend later merely distraught.

Hearst had arranged berths for his Los Angeles-bound guests on a late train Sunday night. They would have a good dinner, a movie, and then be taken to the railroad station at San Luis Obispo. They would reach Los Angeles early Monday morning. Still, Kobler wanted to leave with us.

Again, the services at the Ranch worked smoothly. Our bags were packed; the car ready and waiting at the steps of the castle precisely at five that afternoon, designated by me as the time of departure.

Kobler spent a last hour upstairs in the secluded quarters of his boss. We had to wait for him. I thought he looked a little pale as he climbed into his space behind us. As our car headed away from the castle, he looked back and breathed a sigh, loud and heartfelt.

"No matter how beautiful it is here," he said, "I'm always glad to leave."

Inside the studio walls, twin bungalows were built side by side, for Thalberg and Selznick, as their industrial residences. Their mutual respect was apparent, but beneath the camaraderie they displayed, Kate and I were aware of boiling tensions. It was becoming an intense rivalry, an undeclared war.

At our meetings with Thalberg, he complained that most of the studio's great stars were booked ahead, not only by Selznick but also by his former associates. The productions he wanted to make might have to wait months. He lamented that Selznick had latched onto *Viva! Villa!* for Wallace Beery, even though he had okayed buying the film rights when he ran the studio. It fulfilled the formula he applied when he contemplated box-office possibilities, and in this case the blustery Beery as Mexico's bandit-hero added up to "a star and a title the public will want to see." Almost angrily, he approved the purchase of a melodramatic novel, *China Seas,* and vowed to get it made with Beery if he had to wait years for his availability.

In his next-door bungalow, Selznick complained of the antagonisms he was encountering in "Irving's studio." Mayer was throwing the full force of his influence behind Selznick, but even that wasn't enough to hide the hostilities of department heads, the writers, directors and stars. "There is no way I can win the loyalties of men and women whose whole careers are due to Irving," he mourned. "And I'll never live down my relationship to LB." He had lined up films for the major stars, but Garbo, Gable, Joan Crawford and Jean Harlow were hinting broadly they preferred Thalberg as their producer.

To circumvent the future loss of those stars, Selznick asked us to bring him extensive analyses of literary classics. He wanted large scale canvases that might preclude the need for big stars. He had a preference for the works of Charles Dickens. And by coincidence, Thalberg made the same request, especially stressing a desire for an in-depth study of *Romeo and Juliet*.

Making no secret of his impatience, Thalberg was going off the lot and signed the Marx Brothers, whose movie success skidded downhill through five zany comedies at Paramount. The producer expected to rescue their popularity and was bringing in George S. Kaufman, who helped concoct their early Broadway shows, to assist him.

His wife, Norma Shearer, was exclusively his star. Of course he was greatly heartened when Hearst agreed to trade *Operator 13* for *The Barretts of Wimpole Street*. The moment the trade was finalized, the secret that Norma Shearer would play Elizabeth was revealed for the first time. It was rumored that Hearst was furious and later events confirmed it.

Both films were rushed into production. True to his promise, Mayer secured Gary Cooper for the Civil War comedy while Thalberg settled for lesser luminaries in his period drama.

As was not uncommon in my average day, a noted novelist appeared unannounced at the studio gate and was directed to my office. His tall slender figure seemed to bend in the middle and he spoke with a strong Irish brogue.

Liam O'Flaherty was passing through Hollywood when he decided to add a tour of a studio to his American visit. I agreed to act as his guide but almost instantly regretted it as he embarked on a tirade against movies and movie people. I stifled my desire to discuss which of his writings he looked on as good film possibilities and listened in silence as he lambasted with picturesque Irish curses the entire industry and those involved in it.

Then, ahead of us on the studio street appeared Maureen O'Sullivan, lovely and angelic, wearing a lacy pink outfit with crinoline hoopskirts for her role in *Barretts.*

I broke in on O'Flaherty's maledictions and said, "Here's someone you're sure to like."

"O'Sullivan? Sure an' I know you," he told her. "Jasus, I knew yer mother before you were born. The old biddy never drew a sober breath."

I yanked him away and, holding his arm firmly, headed for the nearest exit. Two days later, Maureen came to my office, a mischievous smile on her face. She had placed a phone call to Ireland to tell her mother what the writer said, but the Transatlantic service was bad and there was a long delay. The phone company was cooperative and alerted the actress' mother she was getting a call from her daughter. She waited it out at the local pub, to which the call was diverted, and when the connection finally came through, she was in no condition to discuss sobriety.

The Barretts of Wimpole Street was Thalberg's first important success after he turned to personal producing, while *Operator 13* was Marion's last failure after having survived many at MGM. When the returns of both films became known, Hearst moved his star off the lot. He had the bungalow carried several miles over the hills from Culver City to Burbank, a relatively simple feat for a man who shipped castles from Europe to California. Love moves mountains, the poets say. Houses are more practical.

Chapter Ten

Upton Sinclair and I kept our friendship that began with the negotiations for *The Wet Parade,* although no producer displayed any interest in his other books. In 1933, he aroused new fears among them because of his "Bolshevik" leanings. He helped raise financing for the Russian director Sergei Eisenstein to film a documentary about poverty in Mexico. It was made in a climate of continuous problems.

In 1934, Sinclair encountered problems of another sort when he decided to run for governor on a platform to end poverty in California. The initials of his plan provided the word EPIC, which he hoped would land him the office.

I had no doubt that he sincerely believed he could accomplish the goal to which he was dedicated. But mainly he appealed to the aged, the poverty-stricken and the beaten. These ragged followers worried the political elite of the state, as well as the top executives of the Hollywood film studios. They set out to do something about it.

Sinclair's opponent was a colorless, indifferent politician, the incumbent governor of California. There were very few good deeds in his record to warrant tossing hats in the air. So, a way to lick Sinclair had to be found in his own campaign. His followers provided the source of their own undoing, as the film industry resorted to a novel method of character assassination.

Newsreels set up cameras in various parts of the state and canvassed voters on their choice. They showed that only the well-dressed intelligentsia spoke in favor of the present governor, Frank Merriam, while squatters in the hobo camps in the railroad jungles of Colton or vagrants on Los Angeles' Skid Row voiced approval of Upton Sinclair. In reality, any tramp who spoke for Merriam landed on the cutting room floor. Well-dressed voters who preferred Sinclair were never seen by the voters, who didn't sense the artful juggling of these newsreel shots.

In addition to this photographic chicanery, the film studios dunned their employees for money to defeat Sinclair. When approached to contribute, I asked what I was expected to give, then sent a check in that sum to Sinclair and the EPIC program. It didn't help.

The newsreels made a mightier contribution to Sinclair's defeat. It helped end worries that "that Bolshevik" might seize the studios and turn them into fashionable homes for the aged. The re-election of Frank F. Merriam to the governorship allowed California to continue his bumbling, inept administration, indicating that Thalberg's hard-line, "I make them do it my way so they'll never know if their way is better," was not just confined to making movies.

Lederer stayed on the writing staff after "Aunt Marion" departed and even after Hecht and MacArthur went back to New York to see their new play *Jumbo* through rehearsals. This gargantuan circus story would carry another nosegay for their adoring friend, a program credit, "Joke by Charles Lederer."

The unidentified joke, which did, in fact, draw the show's biggest laugh from its audiences, occurred when Jimmy Durante was accosted by a sheriff as he was sneaking out of the grounds. The lawman, impowered to seize the circus and all its assets, asked Durante, "Where are you going with that elephant?" The comic, holding a leash attached to a huge pachyderm, asked indignantly, *"What* elephant?"

Meanwhile Moss Hart was perched to take off for a sabbatical from screen writing, intent on inhaling the heady atmosphere of the Broadway theatre. He had truly arrived, and was riding the crest of an assortment of successful plays and movies, all his youthful ambitions achieved. A charming, modest extrovert, he liked to downplay his achievements but was very happy to have achieved them.

Lederer and I collared him for a lunch in the commissary, to speed him on his way as well as to dispute his bizarre belief that writing for the stage had it all over writing for the screen. During that meal, Moss offered us an idea for a movie he had no time to work out. A Broadway gossip columnist invents a girl-about-town he calls Miss Pamela Thorndyke. She has beauty and style and his daily column records her presence at parties, premieres and all the glamorous gathering places he covers. Through his writings she becomes a celebrity although so elusive that he alone, it seems, recognizes her among those present.

The columnist's enjoyment with his deception goes sour when his boss-lady publisher commands that he bring Miss Thorndyke to a big social soiree that she is hostessing. No escape seems possible, his situation is desperate. But just then, Miss Pamela Thorndyke, herself, is announced at the reception desk. In walks a fascinating female who looks exactly as he has been describing her.

That was as far as Moss got with his story. It was also as far as he intended to go. He had no time to develop it in the foreseeable future. Having learned that most good movie ideas could be told in a paragraph, I expressed a liking for it. Lederer agreed.

Pleased with our interest, Moss offered it as a gift. "A tiny gesture for two admired friends who will probably steal it anyway," he said.

We agreed enthusiastically, certain we were well-equipped to flesh out the plot. Falling in with Hart's love of contracting rhetoric, we assured him we could improve on his meager genius, while I, familiar with MGM's story needs, felt it was clearly an unpolished, saleable gem.

It was clear, too, that its value if authored by Lederer and Marx would be minimal, while the name of Moss Hart, much as he hated to admit it, represented real substance in the marketplace. We offered to give Moss sole credit for the story we would write but split the proceeds three ways.

The deal was made and after Moss departed, Lederer and I had a series of lighthearted writing sessions, tossing improbable lines into its directions, some of which, in retrospect, seem brighter than our dialogue. Examples of this were "He hides behind a potted palm and two potted guests," and "Sweating like a horse that just came in last at the Kentucky Derby." We left it to a director to figure out how to film them.

Our completed story line attracted MGM producer John Considine, Jr. He bought it and put three writers and a director to work adapting it into scenario form. During the weeks they slaved at it, Lederer made regular inquiries about their progress. I had to ask him to quit when Considine's writers complained, "Charley Lederer is always snooping around. He is either trying to steal the story or get our jobs."

It went into production for a 1935 showing as *The Broadway Melody of 1936*. Its story by Moss Hart was advertised as "So new it's a year ahead of its time."

The saga of Miss Pamela Thorndyke might have ended there except that soon after the film opened, the story by Moss Hart was nominated for an Academy Award. Lederer and I reacted with serene astonishment as compared to Hart, who greeted the news with total horror.

"I am quietly livid!" he screamed over the phone, so loudly it seemed he hardly needed the instrument. He vowed, if he won, to denounce us as double-crossers who had villainously forced him to win an honor he didn't deserve and wouldn't accept.

Clothed in self-righteous indignation which Lederer and I deplored, Moss waited the fateful moment when the year's winner would be announced. His speech of renunciation was ready for delivery and we fully expected him to use it, for the movie (with Robert Taylor and Eleanor Powell) was a bigger hit with the public than its two competitors for the Oscar. As the evening droned on toward the writing award, three worried individuals sat low in their seats, fearful of the moments ahead. But when the announcement of the winner came, we led the cheers for Ben Hecht and *The Scoundrel.*

Each new film provided inspiration to people prone to sue. Legal claims for damages were the occupational disease of film-makers. There were no vaccinations against them. Many were without merit of any kind, popping out of nowhere after a film's release but commanding attention because the litigant attempted to restrain the exhibition until his case was decided.

These irritations were constant, they were rightly called "nuisances suits" and usually a few dollars would be offered in settlement to avoid the waste of time involved defending them. Quite often, the complainant would take the money and run.

The MGM legal department kept a hot-line sizzling to my office, seeking background on a story or script that was under fire in the courts. In many such instances, the basis of the lawsuit was well suited to comedy.

There was a single sequence in *The Thin Man,* the mystery story by Dashiell Hammett, that prompted such a lawsuit. Nick and Nora Charles, played by William Powell and Myrna Loy, are walking their terrier, Asta, on a city street. Director W. S. Van Dyke artfully moved his camera from a low setup and it focused on Asta's leash as the two actors spoke their dialogue. The perambulating camera would pick up a street hydrant, at which point the leash tightened for a brief interval, the actors halted until the leash relaxed and then their walk continued. The audiences loved the scene, and miniature hydrants went on sale at toy shops as Christmas gifts for canine pets.

An indignant complainant sued, declaring the laughter caused by the scene held him up to ridicule. He claimed to recognize one of the hydrants as standing in front of his residence and he had not been paid for filming it. He nearly won until the studio proved the scene was shot on a standing set on the back lot known as "the New York Street."

The story department had to plead guilty in two cases that were lost and less amusing. Corbaley and I recommended to producer Hunt Stromberg that he star Joan Crawford in a film of Edward Sheldon's melodrama *Dishonored Lady.* He embraced the idea eagerly and was disappointed when the play's purchase was banned by the Motion Picture Association, the industry-supported watchdog group that tried like hell to protect the public from seeing sin in public.

Dishonored Lady dramatized the true story of Madeline Smith, who had removed her lover from among the living so she could marry a rich suitor. Corbaley and I knew the same story had been fictionalized by Marie Belloc-Lowndes as *Letty Lynton,* which was not banned. We disclosed this to Stromberg, who took it from there. But then, in adapting the subject to the screen, the producer added spice to the Belloc-Lowndes version based on fond memories of the spicier play. Evidence of this was clear to all in the completed movie, including the members of the jury that handed over all the film's profits to playwright Sheldon. He, too, had caught the similarities, as did his lawyer.

The second legal diaster to overtake the studio rose up after the release of *Rasputin and the Empress.* It starred a trio of related thespians—John, Lionel, and Ethel Barrymore. The plot was embroidered out of well-known events that swirled about the throne of Imperial Russia.

Just as it was going to be released, the studio's legalites came up with something to discourage the new breed of lawsuit-happy complainants. They demanded that all films carry a declaration that characters on screen were fictitious and any resemblance to persons living or dead was purely coincidental.

"Rasputin is no more fictitious than I," howled Ben Hecht, spokesman for himself and Charlie MacArthur, who did the script. Based on historical facts, they contended that they had goofed if their characters didn't resemble persons living or dead.

The declaration was removed and in its place was the statement that *Rasputin and the Empress* was woven out of facts, thus setting the stage for a major legal disaster.

The screen story claimed incontestably that Rasputin was murdered by Prince Youssoupoff. It seemed only fair to assume that this last living member of the group would prefer not to be branded a murderer, so his name was changed to Chegodieff in the cast listing.

A prominent attorney, Fanny Holtzman, who specialized in entertainment law, sought out Prince Youssoupoff and informed him he had cause for action. Here he was, of royal blood, not getting his rightful credit for a killing he actually did.

Miss Holtzman filed suit in London, where Prince Youssoupoff resided. The English courts agreed that her client wasn't getting his rightful credit as a murderer. The verdict was for one of the largest amounts ever awarded against a movie until that time, and its decision was appeal-resistant.

The Youssoupoff case barely passed into history when a real Prince Chegodieff popped up, fire in his eyes and a complaint in his hands. He sued because he did not do what Prince Youssoupoff did. He won his case, too, and the films after that, including biographies, disclaimed any resemblance to persons living or dead, and if any more Youssoupoffs or Chegodieffs appeared, they could be told it was all a coincidence.

In 1934, Harry Rapf, the veteran producer with the elongated nose, had charge of making the studio's one- and two-reel short films. They provided training for new talent. Offices and schoolrooms on the lot teemed with the bright faces of apprentice writers, directors, and players. One of them was Richard Goldstone, an aspiring author, fresh out of UCLA, where his contributions to *The Bruin,* the college paper, had won him Rapf's approbation and a thirty-dollar-a-week paycheck.

Short subjects used varied ideas—musicals, animation, biographies, historical incidents, and old folk tales. All the eager young participants sought to interest Rapf in their own story notions and, at Goldstone's request, I arranged a meeting for him with Rapf in which he would propose a fanciful story he remembered from childhood.

About twenty minutes after their meeting occurred, Rapf phoned to say the youth had been presenting an appealing idea when he took sick and dashed out the door. He urged me to check on Goldstone's health.

I found the young writer pale and woebegone. "You've got to get me out of this. I forgot what Mr. Rapf looked like, and I started telling him this story about a little boy, and every time he tells a lie his nose grows bigger . . ."

Although Rapf always had compassion for people in trouble, I wasn't anxious to explain Goldstone's predicament. Hinting that the writer was quite ill, I reported he couldn't meet with him in the near future. Rapf extended his sympathies and never asked to hear the rest of the story.

That story, of course, was *Pinocchio,* which was made into an enormously profitable and popular film by Walt Disney five years later.

With Thalberg no longer supervising the program, weekly story meetings ceased. Selecting what movies to make next year became a free-for-all. Corbaley and I scattered our fire, carefully bringing new story possibilities to those producers we thought would show the most interest, while sending synopses of upcoming books and plays to them all. Mayer tried to give new producers a free rein to select what they liked, which resulted in a rising tide of bad films.

In the undeclared rivalry between Selznick and Thalberg, they, too, scored zeroes when each brought forth a pair of still-born attractions. Selznick fathered a musical, *Reckless,* based on his own original idea, and a dull drama by Hugh Walpole, *Vanessa: Her Love Story.* Thalberg made *Riptide,* which he conceived, and remade Michael Arlen's once spicy *The Green Hat,* which proved lamentably unappetizing.

In the early months of 1935, they turned to creations based on more robust material. We had no need to acquire rights for Selznick. From our observation post, Corbaley and I noted his choice of literary classics long in the public domain. He was making Tolstoi's *Anna Karenina* and Dickens's *David*

Copperfield and *A Tale of Two Cities*. They would be the only films he would make at MGM. Producing for him had been a struggle that by this time doused and finally drowned the cheerful persona he had brought to the studio with him. The belief that he had invaded a region loyal and dedicated to Thalberg was very clear and, in a memorandum to Mayer explaining this, he moved out.

Only *The Barretts of Wimpole Street* had so far come off as well as Thalberg's adherents expected of him, but in 1935 he embarked on a series of productions that were in keeping with their expectations. They began with an uncharacteristic venture into the slapsticky world of wild comedy. It would star the Marx Brothers—Groucho, Zeppo and Harpo—who had finished five films at Paramount on a sliding scale of quality, their first one great, their fifth awful. Before signing with Thalberg, they met with him and were impressed with his analysis of what had gone wrong. "Each of your films had the obligatory star-crossed lovers," he said, "but you guys might as well have been in another picture. You go your way as if the love story didn't exist. In my film, you'll provide the help the lovers need to get together. In simpler terms it's called a rooting interest."

The brothers knew, as I did, that we were distantly related but were never able to figure out exactly how. It was no coincidence that their father's name was Samuel; three Samuels, including myself, were strung through my father's side of the family. The day Groucho checked in on the lot, I said, "Well, I finally got some relatives on the payroll." Groucho didn't think it was funny. But the movie they made undeniably was. Playwright George S. Kaufman, architect of the zany musicals that carried them to stage stardom, whipped up *A Night at the Opera*.

Laughs were the neon lights that lit up Kaufman's world. Crisp one-liners radiated from the tall, gaunt Broadwayite with the unforgettable face. Coal-colored hair stood up like a picket fence, his eyes peered searchingly beneath bushy black eyebrows and over his horn-rimmed glasses. Against his dry, cutting wit, few were safe; many of his closest friends were bruised victims.

One who escaped his sarcastic shrapnel was his former collaborator, Morrie Ryskind, who worked with him on the Marx Brothers stage shows in the 1920s. He rejoined Kaufman in writing the new film. Ryskind was already a confirmed Californian, going home to his wife when the day's work was done. However, Kaufman had left his wife, Beatrice, in the east, sharing his nights with all-female partners in bed and all-male partners at the bridge table. They came in many varieties.

An on-again, off-again friendship of sorts prevailed between Kaufman and Herman Mankiewicz. They had been either at war or maintaining a fragile armistice ever since they worked on the drama desk of the *New York Times,* and collaborated on a play, *The Good Fellow.* It closed after six performances. Mankiewicz's other collaboration, on *The Wild Man of Borneo,* was with Marc Connelly. It hardly did as well. As he changed studios, his normal way of life in Hollywood, Mankiewicz placed on his office walls two telegrams sent him by the producer of those shows, announcing their closings. They carried an inscription that Mankiewicz added: THE DEPLORABLE STATE OF THE AMERICAN THEATRE.

When it came to dealing with self-destruction in a humorous way, Herman Mankiewicz had no superior. He was then on the MGM payroll, jumping on and off like it was a moving streetcar.

He plunged himself and Kaufman into disaster by overenthusiastic bidding at one of their bridge games. After the loss of points was scored, Kaufman leaned politely across the table and said, "When did you learn this game? Be specific, Herman. Don't just say this morning. *What time* this morning?"

When Herman returned to the table after a brief visit to the restroom, Kaufman said, "For the first time tonight I know what you held in your hand."

Kaufman's failures on Broadway were rare, but Mankiewicz never praised his hits. This lack of appreciation provoked the playwright to a point where he finally complained about it. Mankiewicz meekly accepted the rebuke. On opening night of his next show Kaufman was handed a telegram. LOVED IT. HERMAN J. MANKIEWICZ. It also bore instructions, "Deliver *before* the curtain rises."

Another writer on *A Night at the Opera* was lyricist Harry Ruby. Angular, hook-nosed, and as able as Mankiewicz to laugh at himself, Ruby's love for rhymes in his lyrics was totally eclipsed by a maniacal devotion to baseball. The chief concern of his partner, composer Bert Kalmar, was that Ruby would quit songwriting if he could play in the big leagues. Their songwriting sessions were cut short on days when Yankee superstar Joe DiMaggio was playing.

That led writer Norman Krasna to ask, "If you saw your father and Joe DiMaggio teetering on the edge of a cliff and could only save one, who would it be?"

"Are you nuts?" yelped Ruby. "My father never batted two hundred the best year of his life."

In this climate of laughs, the Marx Brothers brought fun to the daily doings at the studio. Anecdotes about them abounded. When Thalberg kept them waiting, they touched a match to papers they piled outside his office and fanned the smoke under the doorsill, screaming, "Fire!" in a variety of dialects. It brought the producer out in a hurry.

They called him "Big Chief" and once, after he left them alone in his office, he came back to find them squatting by the fireplace, blanketed like Indians, feathers in their hair, roasting chestnuts, talking gibberish.

But Groucho had a knack of delivering lines like he was making them up and, at times, he did. "He's a fast man with an ad-lib," said Kaufman. "Even when I tell him what to say."

I heard a pure Grouchoism when we went together to the opening of a revue in a barnlike playhouse. The book was bad, its songs and gags fell flat.

We were moving up the aisle after the final curtain when recognition occurred between Groucho and one of the show's writers. The author was leaning his chin and elbows on the revetment at the back of the auditorium like a fighter on the ropes. He blanched at the sight of Groucho.

"What this show needs is a small house," he said, bleakly.

"You'll have one tomorrow night," snapped Groucho.

Circus atmosphere pervaded the stage where *A Night at the Opera* was filmed until the last shot. It wrapped in bedlam and chaos. A prop man made his way to director Sam Wood with a beat-up clarinet which had been bought to be used in the picture but wasn't.

"What do I do with it?" he asked.

"Throw it away," said the director.

"Just a minute," commanded Groucho. "This is MGM. Have it gold-plated. Then throw it away!"

Reports of the lunatic doings on the Marx Brothers set brought unaccustomed smiles to Thalberg's face. His spirits soared and his wry sense of humor reasserted itself.

Director George Cukor asked him to intercede for Luis Bunuel, a European filmmaker who complained that his political activities made it impossible for him to work in Hollywood. "The poor chap's on the industry's blacklist," said Cukor.

"There is no blacklist," replied Thalberg, sternly. Then he added, "But I'll see he's taken off it."

He also recaptured the control he always wanted on all aspects of his movies. "I run a producer's studio," he said, "and there's no room for auteurs." He made that statement to me after I observed pioneer D. W. Griffith seated forlornly in the lobby of Hollywood's Knickerbocker Hotel. The once-great maker of early film masterpieces was broke and jobless. I asked Thalberg to consider him for one of his productions.

"We couldn't get along in a thousand years," was the way he worded his refusal.

He was concerned at the time with increasing quarrels between his associate producer, Albert Lewin, and director Frank Lloyd. Dissension between them on the Santa Catalina Island location of *Mutiny on the Bounty* finally reached such proportions that Thalberg flew over to restore tranquility.

"This picture isn't big enough for Lewin and myself," Lloyd told him. "You'll have to choose between us."

"I'm sorry to hear you say that, Frank," replied Thalberg, "because I'll hate taking you off."

Lloyd and Lewin went back to work and the film proceeded with both men functioning together.

Albert (Allie) Lewin was a former university professor, reported to have uttered the line that Sam and Bella Spewack appropriated for their Hollywood comedy *Boy Meets Girl,* "They hate me here because I have a college education."

Of short stature but large mental facility, he was a popular executive at MGM where, in its earliest days, he had functioned as its story editor.

When *Mutiny on the Bounty* came back to the studio from location, Lewin was asked a favor by his friend John Farrow, a blond Australian charmer, one of the writers who adapted the *Bounty* saga to the screen. A former sailor, Farrow led a life of endless adventures with his two great loves, ships at sea and ladies on land.

His reputation as a lover was enormous, he logged a fantastic score of conquests, none of which he kept secret. But at this time, hoping to expand his sexperiences, he had run aground in his efforts to pursuade two sisters from MGM's acting stock company to go to bed with him at the same time. The girls were more engrossed with psychoanalysis than with him. Unaccustomed to rebuffs, Farrow blamed it on that science, until he learned that Sigmund Freud claimed it supplied a technique whereby sexual resistance could be eliminated.

Armed with this information, Farrow conceived a delightfully bizarre plan. He mentioned to the girls that Dr. Charles Menninger, founder of the prestigious Menninger Psychiatric Clinic in Topeka, Kansas, was an old friend. They dined at

Farrow's bachelor digs whenever the famous analyst visited California. He was due in a week but Farrow couldn't include the girls because he respected Dr. Menninger's wish for privacy. As he anticipated, the girls begged for an introduction and he finally promised to see what he could do. Then, after recruiting Lewin to impersonate the analyst, he told them he had secured an invitation after all. They would dine with the great man and perhaps get a chance to talk to him about their dreams and personal problems.

The stage was set, the cast complete and the two male leads rehearsed the play. The Menninger-Lewin character would indeed grant the girls private sessions, plus instant interpretations of whatever they told him. Then he would tell them they had repressed desires to sleep with Farrow.

Farrow and Lewin barely finished a run-through of their lines when the sisters arrived. But as Farrow opened the door and turned to introduce them, they saw Lewin behind him. Both screamed "Allie!" and went flying into the arms of the producer.

Farrow survived this misadventure happily, marrying Maureen O'Sullivan and fathering three sons and four daughters.

Marriage had to be strong in the minds of all movie writers when a majority of the films produced in Hollywood ended in real or promised matrimony.

Carey Wilson, collaborating with Farrow on *Mutiny,* entered into that joyous state with a flamboyant spectacle.

It took place at the house and garden of his agent, Phil Berg, whose better-known clients included Clark Gable, Wallace Beery and Joan Crawford. Raking in ten percent of their incomes entitled Berg to a living style rivaling any studio mogul. He owned an awesome land yacht built abroad to his specifications, and a huge ocean-going vessel, as well as a million-dollar collection of pre-Columbian art, housed in a separate wing of his home on Sunset Boulevard in Beverly Hills.

With an agent-client relationship that spanned nearly ten years, Wilson decided on Berg's mansion as his ceremonial locale without bothering to ask for it. The first Berg knew of the plan was when he saw Cedric Gibbons and a crew of workmen surveying the grounds. They were planning to drain and cover the swimming pool, dismantle the tennis court and clear an area that would accommodate the invited guests, described by the *Los Angeles Times* as "more than 500, the elite of filmdom."

Art Director Gibbons explained to the surprised agent that Wilson wanted the area transformed to "slightly resemble the garden of Versailles." He was constructing an altar that would be suffused in a botanical display rivaling England's Kew Gardens; it would include some rare species of orchids Wilson was endeavoring to acquire as a wedding gift from his friend, screen writer Jules Furthman, whose greenhouses were highly visible on a hill behind the studio. However, Furthman maintained that he had been forced to make a business rule not to give away any blossoms for free lest he be swamped by requests from studio executives with wives and/or girlfriends. Wilson rejected Furthman's suggestion he buy the orchids at a discount, as "a crude attempt to profit by my wedding."

Wilson had to cope with another problem when all those with invitations to the wedding received a telegram from a jewelry firm, Brock and Company, stating that the bride, actress Carmelita Geraghty, had selected a crest they had specially designed for her and requested that all gifts for her be purchased at their Beverly Hills shop. A flood of declining RSVPs poured in, forcing the jewelers to send a follow-up wire disassociating themselves from an overeager salesman.

On the sunny spring day of the wedding, May 6, 1935, only about 100 of the "elite of filmdom" showed up.

Marie and I were pleasantly bedazzled to find ourselves in such an exclusive group. Cedric Gibbons and his men had wrought a glamorous and artistic setting in the orchidless but flower-bedecked arbor, camouflaging Phil Berg's swimming pool and tennis court.

The tall, stately bride was the daughter of old-time screen writer, Tom Geraghty, who wrote many of the elder Douglas

Fairbanks's silent films. Her bridesmaid, Jean Harlow, gave the bride and her attendants tulle frocks and picture hats. Unknown to Berg, the captain and crew of his yacht, anchored in Long Beach Harbor, had been uniformed entirely at the agent's expense. Their new outfits had HONEYMOON CRUISE emblazoned on their chests. They were waiting to take the bride and groom to Catalina Island.

Jean Harlow was married to cinematographer Hal Rosson, who was noticeably absent. She kept smiling and winking at the press corps seated in the front row of guests as the minister spoke thoughtfully of the sanctity of marriage. She chose that time to say to the reporters, "Do you fellows know I'm getting a divorce?" In traditional fashion, they raced for the phones.

There was no throwing of rice when the bride and groom departed, because they were the last to leave, long after darkness set in. Then they raced for the harbor in Jean Harlow's limousine, with a police escort leading the way. But while en route, the chauffeur overran one of the motorcycles, tumbling its rider onto the street, whereupon another officer beat up the chauffeur. As an ambulance carried both injured men to a hospital, Wilson drove his bride to the harbor, where she collapsed. The honeymoon cruise never left port.

Monday morning's headlines blared out Harlow's news, SCREEN STAR AND MATE PARTED. It eclipsed the tidings of the wedding but enhanced the public's view of the irrationally romantic world of entertainment. Once again, Marie pronounced it to be her kind of party, while Phil Berg probably had a different assessment. He said it cost him fifteen thousand dollars.

Chapter Eleven

As I neared the end of my first five years at the story post, creative personnel in the studio steadily increased. The writing staff doubled. Many of the newcomers were freelance authors engaged to write a single screenplay. Long-term contracts were becoming obsolete.

This change was largely due to the trials and errors of new producers invited by Louis B. Mayer, always looking for another Thalberg to handle the over-all program. Cynical James K. McGuinness, once a New York newspaper columnist, was making the transition from writer to production executive. He represented Thalberg at Mayer's periodic meetings, which grew so crowded that McGuinness called them "the College of Cardinals." For a time they met early in the morning and the name changed to "The Dawn Patrol." It was thought that an early start would speed production, but these assemblies reverted to a more sober hour when McGuinness, noting the droopy-eyed men around him, said bitingly, "Let's not confuse insomnia with industry!"

In our own sessions, Corbaley and I focused on story decisions that we thought arguable. She still favored "trash" as her favorite descriptive word and on occasions used her influence with Mayer to visit him privately and protest the making of movies she thought would demean the studio's reputation for quality. She could claim several victories along this line; several new producers were stunned when their announced projects were suddenly aborted without explanation. The release of films made in late 1934 and early 1935 was strung into

1936. Big pictures by the older producers kept the standards high. Hunt Stromberg turned out *The Great Ziegfeld, Treasure Island,* and *Ah, Wilderness.* Harry Rapf successfully teamed Myrna Loy and an actor who had been fired from Fox as untalented and impossible, making a star of Spencer Tracy in *Whipsaw.* Bernie Hyman's *San Francisco* shook up theatres everywhere with its earthquake scenes. As he emerged from its preview, a beaming Louis B. Mayer said, "That's my idea of a prestige picture!"

Our respect for Thalberg kept us from raising our voices against his choices. The closest we came to that was back in 1932 when he approved four writers to help Director Tod Browning concoct a horror film called *Freaks.* As it neared production, Siamese twins, misshapen dwarfs, and other human abnormalities were on display in the studio, turning heads and stomachs. At a meeting of Thalberg's friends in Harry Rapf's office, a protest against making the movie was discussed, but Director Jack Conway shot down a march on the producer's office when he said, "Irving's right so often he's earned the right to be wrong."

There was no question in Corbaley's mind that he would be wrong to present Norma Shearer as Juliet in Shakespeare's immortal romance. In the memorandum we received from him, he said it would be the most authentic version ever attempted on the screen. His use of "authentic" provoked her uncontrolled laughter.

"How can he star a thirtyish wife and mother in the role of a fourteen-year-old virgin?" she demanded of me, then said scathingly, "Authentic! Hah!"

To fortify myself against any show of ignorance, I spent that evening with a copy of the play and next morning teased Corbaley with quotations from the text: "If love be blind it cannot hit the mark," "Passion lends them power" and "Love is a smoke raised with the fume of sighs."

"There are quotations to fit any argument," my learned associate replied. "But you needn't worry. I know better than to tell Irving what I think about this."

Movie history was replete with films in which a producer starred the woman he loved. The Hearst-Davies affair was there for us to see close at home. By the very fact of love itself, moviemakers believed the allure they could see must be appreciated by everyone. In Thalberg's eyes, his wife's age was a minor discrepancy in the making of *Romeo and Juliet.* Other than that, he intended to follow the play with utmost integrity. To insure that, he wanted the most eminent Shakespearean authority in America, Professor William Strunk of Cornell University, for the film's technical advisor.

Negotiations over the long-distance phone revealed Strunk was eager for the job. But the deal hit a snag over terms. He was asking the studio to pay him a four-hundred-dollar salary. Thalberg called it highway robbery. No professor in the world, he declared, gets that kind of money. His authority was the resident intellectual, Allie Lewin, who knew collegiate economics.

I was headed east to scout writers and stories and Thalberg asked me to see if I could strike a fair deal with Professor Strunk. He suggested I offer a hundred and fifty dollars, which was Hollywood's going rate for technical advisers. "If necessary, give him two hundred," he said. "After all, he is special."

From New York I phoned Strunk upstate in Ithaca. He asked me to talk to the dean of Cornell, which was okay. It was in the Hollywood tradition—the dean would act as his agent.

He flatly disagreed with me that professors do not receive four-hundred-dollar salaries as a common thing. They do, he stated. And in this case, some of the professor's money would go to remunerate other professors who would fill in for him while he was in Hollywood.

I tried to work it out, agreeing that Professor Strunk's remuneration could be sent directly to the university to do with it as they pleased. I agreed that we thought Professor Strunk was the best man we could get for the job and we wanted him very much. But I couldn't agree about the salary. I took it on myself to offer two hundred dollars. The dean turned it down.

Our back-and-forth haggling was coming to an ignominious end when he said, "I assure you many professors are paid four hundred dollars a *month!*"

I gulped and told him I would think it over and call him back. Throughout our talk, I had been trying to give him eight hundred dollars a month while he was fighting for four! Of course, the studio paid by the week; the college by the month.

After a suitable passage of time I called him back, having fabricated what to say.

"Mr. Thalberg thinks Professor Strunk will find it difficult to live in Hollywood on four hundred a month. He wants him to have six hundred so he'll be comfortable."

The dean was delighted with Thalberg's fairness. In fact, everyone was delighted, including Professor Strunk, who soon learned how different life could be in Hollywood. Soon after he arrived, he had his salary raised to eight hundred a month.

The professor's monetary habits broadened but other traits persisted, narrowed by his collegiate training. Told he could have all the stationery his arms could carry, he never asked for it. Instead, he would wait until after business hours, when he tiptoed to the cabinet where it was kept, carefully extracted a single letterhead and envelope, and ran like a rabbit.

Charming and delightful, Strunk had theories about the mystery surrounding the authorship of William Shakespeare's plays. He believed the plays resulted from a collaboration by the regulars who patronized London's Mermaid Tavern. He likened their writing to the methods of the studio.

"Certainly, he cultivated the intellectuals," he told me. "They knew the plots of the old Italian novellas, they laid out the story lines, but Bill Shakespeare was part owner of the Globe Theatre and he had to have plays to keep the place going, so he helped them turn in material. He rewrote their stuff to make it work in his theatre, but they didn't have agents or a writer's guild, there were no royalties to be paid and therefore the credit for authorship wasn't important. So they let him have it."

He claimed he could pinpoint lines that Shakespeare contributed to each play, though some of the poorer ones had none by the master and some better ones were entirely his. "He had to have a new show for his customers the way movie companies do now," he said. "He was a showman and would have probably made the best movie producer in history."

Novelists, as I often noted, had a penchant for depicting the fun and pleasure that precedes war and tragedy. But in the summer of 1936 no one in the studio knew what was coming. In all aspects, it was a make-believe world.

In that year, the analogy between reality and fiction didn't occur to me. I was busier than ever, catering to the new producers brought in by hard-driving Louis B. Mayer. They came and went as if the front gate was a revolving door. Corbaley had known far more changes of studio command than I and she was far more philosophical about it.

"Relax and enjoy," she advised, adding that eternal truism, "Even this shall pass." I took her suggestion to heart, knowing how wisely she always counseled. There weren't many parties to attend but then, the times themselves had a jolly aspect.

Each day, the mail department dropped a mixed bag on my desk. Ideas for movies were the common theme. A journalist in Wilkes-Barre, Pennsylvania, wrote briefly and to the point.

> *From the town that gave Hollywood Herman Mankiewicz, Samson Raphaelson and Louis Weitzenkorn comes the best idea of the year. Do the life of Irving Berlin. Send check to Mike Bernstein.*

I was answering all sensible letter-writers, and Bernstein couldn't be faulted as off this mark.

Lives of modern composers, real or imagined, offered entertaining opportunities for songs and dances. Every studio in town toyed with a presentation of Irving Berlin's career but a check for doing it would have to go to the composer and not a proposer. Instead of explaining this, I relaxed and enjoyed and wrote back:

> *Sorry I can't send check but I'm sending Herman Mankiewicz, Samson Raphaelson and Louis Weitzenkorn.*

Another applicant sent a letter seeking a job as technical adviser on stories laid in mythical kingdoms, because, as he wrote, "I've lived most of my life in them."

"Me, too," I told Corbaley.

We enjoyed hearing a pitch from an agent whose writer-client suggested Jules Verne's *Twenty Thousand Leagues Under the Sea,* and then, sensing uncertainties in our response, he added, "You can always change the background." And a story on the life of Queen Marie of Roumania was rejected by a producer who said, "I don't like mythical kingdom stories."

H. G. Wells, whose imagination made mythical kingdoms come to life, was a houseguest of Charles Chaplin. Called on to make a speech to a group of writers, he rose from his chair to say, "Hollywood leaves me speechless," and sat down.

Real-life stories were all-important, and Robert Noble submitted an idea taken from life—his own. He had occupied the guest house of a married couple and when they went to court for a divorce, both named him as correspondent. But the industry censors took a dim view of his romance and banned what might have been a sophisticated comedy like those of Noel Coward.

Noel Coward passed through Hollywood and was the houseguest of John Gilbert. The day after he left, Gilbert celebrated with a stag affair, to which I was invited. He was less than enchanted with the playwright. Gilbert lived high in many ways, on a hilltop, three previous marriages on the rocks. Despite those disasters and the crash of his career on the hidden shoals of sound, he was an affable and attractive host, enlivening the party with an account of the week just passed.

Noel Coward was not a personal friend. He had been a stranger to him until the visit, given shelter at the request of mutual acquaintances. The playwright was in California waiting the ship that would take him to the Orient, and during that week Gilbert threw a party in honor of his guest. He reported what happened when the house emptied.

Gilbert and Coward relaxed by the fireplace, drinking.

"I was flattered, the way he thanked me. It was embarrassing. He kept saying he hoped our acquaintanceship would flower into a close friendship." Then, Gilbert related, "I suddenly realized he was drawing his chair closer. I hardly noticed his hand on my knee, but when it started slowly crawling toward my crotch, I knew I had to do something about it. But what? Here's a great man, a guest in my house, putting me on a hell of a spot. I couldn't insult him but I was getting panicky. I looked at his hand and then laughed uproariously in his face. I howled. He got the message. He jumped up huffily and went off to his room."

Not long after Gilbert's party, I was alone in my office, working late. As often happens during southern California's dry season, the rain was coming down in torrents—a good night to wade through the deluge of reading matter on my desk. Then, above the storm, I heard the outer-office screen door open and, quite appropriately, the author of the play *Rain* appeared.

The liquid skies had doused John Colton externally, the contents of a bottle did the same internally. He lurched toward me.

"Saw the light," he said. His face was flushed as I had never seen it before. "Hope you don't mind . . ."

The mountain of synopses was down to a respectable level and I rather welcomed the interruption. He sat his dripping body down carefully in a chair near me.

Colton had numerous credits through the years, ranging

from the adventurous *White Shadows in the South Seas* to musicals and torrid dramas. He was currently wrestling with an American Indian novel, *Laughing Boy,* that was stubbornly resisting adaptation to the screen. I was aware of the problem and commiserated with him. As I spoke I noticed that he was gazing at me with a strange look of inquiry. He mumbled something in a low voice about wanting to know me better. I was too distant, he said, and as I leaned closer to hear him better I suddenly felt his hand on my knee. It was moving gently upward.

Gilbert's entanglement with Coward flashed through my mind, along with his remedy for this same predicament. I looked at his hand, and attempted to laugh uproariously in his face, as the actor had. But I couldn't. I couldn't howl. I couldn't match Gilbert's histrionic ability to create hilarity on cue.

Panicked, I jumped up, pushed past the playwright and ran into the storm, sloshing through the flooded street, ignoring hoarse cries to wait, comforted by knowing he was in no shape to follow.

The Labor Day holiday always seemed to me the least joyous holiday of the year, perhaps because it marked the end of summer and signaled the coming of winter. As September 7, 1936, approached, director Robert Z. Leonard invited Marie and me to spend it with a convivial studio group at Del Monte. Leonard was a great bear of a man, at the apex of a lengthy career that began in the silent movie era.

Thalberg came along with Norma Shearer, who had completed *Romeo and Juliet.* The next story readied for her was *Marie Antoinette,* which her producer-husband didn't want to make then because he didn't want her to appear in successive costume pictures.

"Let's talk about something modern for Norma in between."

I brought along a list of new books and plays, but our meetings were postponed through the holiday weekend when he came down with a cold and stayed in bed.

He stayed in bed when he got home, but then left it to go to the Hollywood Bowl to assist in staging *Everyman,* a visionary pageant that pleaded for religious tolerance. It rained all that week but he shook off the pleadings of his wife and friends to let others handle the staging, claiming it was an obligation he wanted to fulfill. The public performance was to be Wednesday night, September 16, the eve of the Jewish New Year 5697. Each night he returned from the Bowl his cold was worse, diagnosed now as influenza.

Monday morning, September 14, I strolled through the studio with Kate Corbaley. We were still searching for a modern vehicle for Norma Shearer. Thalberg wanted an important story in keeping with the other films on the program. He had *Camille* in production with Greta Garbo, and *The Good Earth* with Paul Muni and Luise Rainer. He was planning to make Sinclair Lewis's *It Can't Happen Here* and Franz Werfel's *Forty Days of Musa Dagh.* The best material for Shearer, we decided, was *Forever,* by Mildred Cram, but its illicit love story faced enormous censorship problems.

"He's licked censors before," I said.

When I returned to my office, my secretary looked at me strangely.

"Did you hear about Mr. Thalberg?" she asked.

I shook my head.

"He died."

It must have been that I didn't want to think the unthinkable because it flashed into my mind that I hadn't seen Irving's father for some time.

"You mean William?" I asked.

"No," she said. "Irving."

Chapter Twelve

S amuel Goldwyn navigated the course of his days a completely free soul, in no way influenced, controlled or guided by others. He was a most independent movie producer, undeniably the most important in the world. I was flattered when he asked me to come see him. Facing this genial, smiling movie-industry colossus, I was beguiled by his attractive manners. His offer of a two-year contract at a high salary was undeniably attractive, too.

In 1937, after the confusion that followed Thalberg's death had faded at MGM, I told Louis B. Mayer I wanted out of the story department.

"It wasn't my idea in the first place," I said. "I came here to write." He sympathized with my complaint that pressures of the job sidelined other activities but reacted incredulously at my urge to write. "I'll make you a producer," he said. "You'll be a boss of writers."

I turned Corbaley and the story department over to Edwin Knopf, brother of book publisher Alfred Knopf, and was assigned the making of low-budget movies, the studio's usual training ground for neophytes in all categories. I chose two mystery novels that could be made within the scope of their restrictive costs. The first one was awful; the second a toss-up between awful and passable.

"It's surprising that Mayer allows me to go on," I told Marie.

"I don't think mysteries are your cup of tea," she said.

"With all that story experience, you must know something better kicking around."

Something better kicking around was a play, *Skidding,* that I had seen in New York's Little Theatre before we went to Hollywood. Author Aurania Rouverol had yet to find a movie buyer for her comedy-drama of a small-town judge and his family. I had to overcome the arguments of my executive producer Lucien Hubbard, who had a theory that small-town stories spawned small-time profits. But he finally caved in and the movie was shooting on a back-lot street when Mayer liquidated Hubbard's unit and dispersed its personnel.

He asked me to return to the top spot in the story department. "An oblique way of telling me to forget producing," I told Marie. To go back to my previous job would be a step to the rear but there was no need to consider that because it was then that Goldwyn, with superb timing, dangled his contract. I called and told him we had a deal.

Moving out of a giant studio and into a relatively small organization loomed ahead as a pleasant change. Goldwyn's reputation for respecting good writing talent dated back to the silent movie era, when he had formed the Eminent Authors Company and recruited men and women who fitted that description. Their output was expected to lift movie standards but it fell flat after a few productions. However, he deserved plaudits for trying.

"I want you to write and produce films for me," he said at our first meeting. When I reported for those duties he escorted me to the offices of his staff and introduced me to everyone with a high-pitched laugh that sometimes rose to a cackle. They greeted me warmly, like a newly arrived guest at a party who would share their fun and happy times.

Later, I looked back at some ominous portents ignored in the euphoria of that tour. Associate Producer Merritt Hulburd, a former editor of the *Saturday Evening Post,* lowered his booming voice to a dulcet tone when he said, "Welcome to Little Big Horn," mysteriously evoking the image of Custer's

Last Stand. Goldwyn's other associate producer, George Haight, who had presented a few inauspicious Broadway plays in his pre-Hollywood career, kept a sage piece of advice framed on his office wall: NEVER LOSE YOUR TASTE FOR CHEAP FOOD.

The most ominous of all failed to register when Goldwyn steered me into my own office.

"The first thing I ask you to do," he said, "is find four stories for the pictures I will make. You had to find fifty at MGM every year so in a month you can find four for me."

That made sense, mathematically at least. And it didn't make sense to turn down a request from my employer the first day on the job. I had been steered back to the very work I sought to escape. Later, when I reflected on the events of 1937, I felt that I worked ten years for Samuel Goldwyn one year.

The legendary moviemaker personally financed the films he made and therefore qualified as a man who put his money where his mouth was. But his mouth was creating the greatest legend about him. He punctuated his conversations with fractured phrases. "Include me out," and "In two words, impossible," were among those that gained him a curious kind of fame. He far outdid Sheridan's Mrs. Malaprop as a misuser of the language. The term "Malapropisms" was being replaced around the world by "Goldwynisms."

The subject of Goldwynisms was first mentioned in the little shack that housed the studio restaurant where I lunched with Hulburd, Haight, and casting executive Fred Kohlmar. They solemnly informed me that I wouldn't merit acceptance until I heard the boss say some suitable nonsequitur.

It happened almost immediately.

I was walking on the lot with Goldwyn when he introduced me to a contract player whom he called Joe McCrail.

Good-naturedly, the actor said, "My name isn't Joe McCrail. It's Joel McCrae."

Equally good-natured, Goldwyn said, "Look, *he's* telling *me* how to say his name and I've got *him* under contract."

I approached our first story conference in a state of high elation, bearing a new manuscript by A. J. Cronin, *The Citadel.*
No other studio had seen it. But no sooner did I start to picture
the drama of a doctor locked in a struggle against hospital
traditions than Goldwyn stopped me. He had once produced
a picture about a doctor and was surprised that I would suggest
another. That picture, Sinclair Lewis's *Arrowsmith,* he recalled,
had lost him a fortune.

"But you are new here, you don't know," he reflected, not
unkindly "Now I make a rule for you. No doctor stories."

MGM produced *The Citadel.*

At the next meeting he rejected Louis Bromfield's *The
Rains Came.* It was set in India and he had produced a movie
about India in 1924. He said it lost money. "I make a rule for
you," he said. "No India stories."

Twentieth Century-Fox produced *The Rains Came.*

An English playwright, H. M. Harwood, submitted a romance set in a mythical kingdom. I didn't even get around to
the plot, just a short preface, the way Corbaley would have
done.

"I make a rule as long as you work for me," he broke in.
"No mythical kingdom stories."

Soon after that, producer David Selznick previewed a
swash-buckling romance in a mythical kingdom, *The Prisoner
of Zenda.* The Hollywood trade papers praised it and I was
summoned to Goldwyn's office.

"Do you know *Graustark?*" he asked. I told him that I did.
A best-seller years before, it was a romantic potboiler, distantly
related to the heroics of the new Selznick film. The source of
Goldwyn's inspiration wasn't hard to figure out.

"I'd like you to buy it for me," he said.

Graustark had been filmed as a silent picture by Joseph M.
Schenck, who had no interest in refilming it.

Goldwyn approved Schenck's asking price and in a short

time I told him he had become the proud owner of its film rights, the first positive acquisition since my arrival. He expressed pleasure, but with reservations.

"You are my story editor, aren't you?"

"I'm afraid I am," I admitted.

"But who suggested *Graustark?*"

"You did, Mr. Goldwyn."

"But you're my story editor. Why didn't you?"

I said that would have meant breaking his rule. I reminded him he had declared mythical kingdom stories taboo and Graustark was a mythical kingdom. He thought about that a moment.

"I remember," he said, "but I didn't mean *classics!*"

He never made *Graustark.*

John Ford was directing *Hurricane,* a South Seas saga by the writers of *Mutiny on the Bounty.* Ford had an indomitable determination to make pictures his way and a reputation for living any way that it pleased him to live. The violent behavior that he depicted in his films and lived off-screen was the envy of similarly-inclined contemporaries who couldn't match his free-spirited attitude.

Ford's reputation wasn't lost on Goldwyn, who made a cryptic request to his top echelon to meet him in a projection room late one night. Only after the door was locked did he explain that we were to see a rough cut of *Hurricane* in order to get a feeling about it from the footage already assembled. It seemed to him the better part of discretion to keep this nocturnal peep show from the director.

The screening revealed an insight into Goldwyn's expertise at analyzing a film's shortcomings whenever he saw its scenes projected before his eyes. Viewing the incomplete *Hurricane,* he was distressed by a lack of close-ups of Dorothy Lamour and Jon Hall, who were playing its two lovers. How to solve that problem was now compounded by another, how to tell John Ford.

Again pledging us to secrecy, he said he would figure out

a solution at home in bed. Next morning, Goldwyn suggested we take a stroll on the lot. Suddenly he pushed open the heavy metal door to the stage where *Hurricane* was shooting. The company was working in a thatched hut set on the far side, diagonally across from where we entered.

We barely took a step forward when Ford's voice bellowed across the dark distance, "What do you want?"

Goldwyn stopped abruptly.

When his question went unanswered, Ford shouted, "You, Mr. Goldwyn! What do you want?"

We stood mute and rooted as he came toward us.

Goldwyn's voice was timid and apologetic. "I've been thinking, Jack, that maybe you should make some more close-ups."

Ford glared pugnaciously at him. "You'll get all the close-ups you need," he said, and used the flat of his hand to measure Goldwyn's waist. "From here up."

Goldwyn backed away and Ford moved with him.

"Or from here." This time Ford's hand struck high on Goldwyn's chest.

Then he clenched his fist and said, "Or from here!" He shook his fist in Goldwyn's face.

Goldwyn wheeled and left the stage. As we headed back to his office, he said, "Well anyway, I put it in his mind."

Goldwyn's only other movie being shot at that time was *The Adventures of Marco Polo.* Its star, Gary Cooper, accepted as director a quiet and unassuming fellow, cinematographer Rudy Mate, who was directing his first film and much too happy with this change of career to make waves.

No more was said about close-ups in *Hurricane* but after viewing new scenes, even without close-ups, the producer voiced his opinion that only tough directors who were uncompromising bastards made great movies. He claimed he preferred men who argued with him. His penchant for removing directors from films when they were in production was constant and his record for that distinction exceeded all his contemporaries. However, he proved his theory about toughness for on their completion, *Hurricane* was successful and *Marco Polo* was not.

The screen writer of Polo's historic trek was the mildest of men, seven-footer Robert Emmet Sherwood, who began his literary career as a film critic and blossomed into one of America's better playwrights.

For a future assignment, Sherwood recommended a classic story he remembered from boyhood and Goldwyn agreed to consider filming it. A copy of the book was found in a children's bookstore. It was in oversized type with colored lettering. The story was set in a mythical kingdom but because Sherwood recommended it Goldwyn promised to read it anyway.

Three weeks later, Sherwood dropped by to see how Goldwyn liked the story. Goldwyn reported he was enjoying it immensely and eager to see how it came out.

"How far are you?" asked Sherwood.

Goldwyn had reached page four. He still had most of it unread when MGM bought *The Wizard of Oz*.

Freddy Kohlmar would bounce into my office to say, "The boys are meeting at Lucey's tonight," then scoot away as though fearful there were devils in pursuit.

Lucey's was a restaurant and bar on Melrose Avenue in Hollywood, built like an Italian grotto with two rows of crypts, not unlike catacombs, enclosed by curtains that shielded the occupants from prying eyes. Eve, a buxom lady, guarded the doorway and the telephone switchboard, sweetly turning away anyone seeking information about errant wives, workers, husbands, or lovers. With eyes that saw all and lips that said nothing, Eve's trustworthiness could be surmised by the truckload of Christmas gifts bestowed on her each year by grateful customers.

To my new associates, grievances against the boss were part of normal existence, mixed with grudging admissions that life with Goldwyn wasn't all bad. They acknowledged that he paid well for the indignities he heaped upon them, but Fred Kohlmar contended Goldwyn's pay had no sticking power. "Take my case," he said. "I have enough saved to live comfortably the rest of my life, providing I don't live more than three weeks."

This particular meeting was to discuss Alva Johnston, an investigative biographer for the *Saturday Evening Post* who was permitted to roam the lot for an article on Goldwyn. In his interviews with us, he seemed anxious to collect as many Goldwynisms as possible. What do do about them called for important consideration.

The group was fiercely protective of their chief's great standing as a creator of language howlers because a serious rival had surfaced overseas. Hungarian producer-director Alexander Korda was achieving some matching fame, currently quoted as saying, "Men like me don't grow on trees."

"I wish Goldwyn had thought of that," said Kohlmar.

True Goldwynisms were easily spotted by experts in the field. Authentic quotes always carried some indication of what he meant. But they were also easy to falsify. Bogus Goldwynisms flooded the town like counterfeit paintings in a flea market. It was decided that Alva Johnston, wide-eyed from Philadelphia, was unlikely to detect the false from the real and a few must be immediately invented in order to protect the reputation of the boss.

Suggested, tested and argued against were "Why should I put my head in a moose?" and "It rolls off my back like a duck." No one believed in the authenticity of a report that when he saw a sun dial, Goldwyn asked, "What will they think of next?" Seasoned Goldwyn watchers easily spotted such artificiality.

We approved a rumor that on hearing that a new father named his son John, Goldwyn complained, "Every Tom, Dick and Harry is named John." It was donated to Alva Johnston's

Saturday Evening Post story, which grew to become a book, *The Great Goldwyn*. He described Goldwyn's language twisters as unrivalled, stating "Sam does not enjoy his preeminence although at times he has deliberately promoted it." His book pulled no punches detailing the producer's bad manners and reported that "the crack novelists he surrounds himself with study him like a strange sociological specimen." Perusing the piece, I concluded that if it had appeared earlier I would have had serious doubts before I entered the domain of this highly acclaimed filmmaker.

One of "the boys" who joined us at our conclaves at Lucey's was Lillian Hellman, then the only writer on Goldwyn's staff. She was adapting Sidney Kingsley's melodrama *Dead End,* and in the congenial atmosphere of those meetings, Lillian and I observed an undeclared truce in the war that had raged between us since we first knew each other.

But in my mind were images similar to flashbacks in movies, detailing episodes that were part of our earlier life.

Ours was a pre-Hollywood acquaintanceship, a case of lovelessness at first fight, a constant duel between two antibodies that would never blend.

Lillian was a skinny, bony slip of a girl before our gaudy spree of the 1930s. She had rust-colored, bobbed hair and an unpretty face that was in a state of perennial indignation about the human condition. To her, every cause was good, there were no bad ones. Just the fact it was a cause made it worthy of support. She voiced that belief at our first meeting and I said, "When people keep a closed mind it suffocates their reason." Looking back at that now, I can see why it would hardly endear me to her.

The link between us was my friendship with her husband, Arthur Kober. An unassuming chap, he was an oddity in the Shubert press department, made up of a whole circus of performing extroverts. Kober had a sly sense of humor and a droll personality, which is why I can't guarantee the truth of his story of how he came to marry Lillian. Lillian wouldn't discuss it, but then she almost never discussed her life with Kober, before or after their marriage.

Like most fellows employed as a Shubert press agent, Kober hoped to be a producer. (Jed Harris was one who made it big for a while.) He put on *Me,* a play by fellow Shubert publicist Henry Myers. Despite its miniscule title, its tiny cast and infinitesimal budget, he had a monumental problem getting it all together.

"Lillian's father offered to back my show if I'd marry his daughter," he said, but he had an escape clause and could buy his way out if the play showed a profit.

Me opened and closed three hours later and Lillian Hellman became Mrs. Arthur Kober, a name she never used. It wasn't my notion of an ideal marriage custom but I wasn't married then and considered it none of my business.

Lillian and I had engaged in our first skirmishes in Lindy's and Reuben's, the popular delicatessens that we favored after theatre curtains came down. We kept on arguing while I walked them to their West Fifty-fifth Street apartment.

Instead of grabbing a subway uptown then, I could sleep on the couch in their parlor. Next morning in the breakfast nook, Lillian and I continued where we left off, triggering that chemical malfunction that was never cured. Whether we had opinions about politicians or show business characters, it was always the same, she liked those I disliked or I liked those she disliked. I don't recall a single instance of agreement between us.

Kober either laughed at us or held his tongue. I was never sure whose side he was on. He smirked at me when she called me a Jewish Cossack and grinned at her when I said she was a Parlor Pink from a very luxurious parlor. Those epithets appeared to sting but we often laughed at them. Laughter was the glue that kept our friendship from reaching a breaking point, even when stretched to its limits.

Light-heartedness was Arthur's most visible characteristic. He had no rapport with Lillian's fondness for rage and he never displayed anger, even when she flaunted her romantic feelings for other men. It was only after they moved to Hollywood and Kober had become a screen writer that the marriage began to fray; the affinity between the passionate and the passive was coming apart. One day he dropped into my office at MGM and asked for help.

"Lillian is bored in California," was how he put it. "She's going to leave me if something isn't done. She's a very talented reader."

Before coming west, Lillian worked as a reader, not only for producer Herman Shumlin but also for publisher Horace Liveright. We were in need of a reader and I gave him a book for her to synopsize. She passed the routine test with honors, her built-in intelligence and experience rated high over all other seekers for the job.

She was paid the standard salary of fifty dollars a week and was a model reader for a few days. Then she swung wildly at the department's peace and contentment. She went about its destruction with the joy a child might show while swinging a baseball bat in a toy shop.

She suggested her fellow workers demand high pay although it was also the standard pay of junior writers. She called on readers to strike for shorter hours and the organization of a union. She made anticapitalistic speeches during lunch hours, at which some agreed with her and others walked away. Inexplicably, she thought they should demand better working conditions although the library-like atmosphere of the department was just what they wanted.

The first to come to me to object to her actions was department head Dorothy Pratt, who called Lillian "uncontrollable," but I laughed her out of it with the help of Kate Corbaley, whose affiliation with readers was closer than mine. She thought Lillian's call for revolution "hilarious."

One of the readers wanted no part of Lillian's passion for change. His name seemed familiar to her, her rampant curiosity caused her to investigate him and when he refused to talk to her, she came to me, eyes gleaming with excitement.

"Do you know who's in that department?"

I assured her I did.

"Wilson Follett!"

Tall and austere, Follett struck me as an impressive individual, cultured and rather remote. His well-composed synopses always carried perceptive comments about movie possibilities.

"What about him?"

"There's a thousand dollar literary prize for a short story he wrote waiting for him in New York that he never picked up. I tried telling him about it but he won't let me."

Considering Follett's salary, this money seemed worth bringing to his attention, so after she left I summoned him. I barely mentioned what Miss Hellman had told me when he interrupted.

"If she doesn't stay away from me I won't be responsible for the consequences."

"Don't you want that money?"

Follett drew himself very erect and said, "It isn't worth it to me." He studied me for a moment, then added, "May I talk to you man-to-man?"

I saw no reason why not.

"I've run away from my wife, a dreadful termagant. You may understand my feelings when I tell you that in order to be free of her I had to abandon my daughter. But I'll never go back. I'm living with a wonderful woman. We are very happy. The reading department presents me with a perfect hiding place which I need because my wife is still looking for me. She has no idea where to find me. If Miss Hellman notifies the Awards Committee where I am, or tries to get that money for me, I promise you I'll . . . I'll . . ."

He closed his fingers together as if he relished the thought of strangulation, turned, and abruptly walked out.

I told Lillian to drop the Follett matter. I also suggested she cut down her political activities within the department. She objected, reminding me that we never agreed in the past and it was no surprise that we were on separate sides now.

Soon after that, Dorothy Pratt had a violent confrontation with Lillian, accusing her of creating an unreasonable amount of unrest in a reasonably tranquil group of people, then came to me and said, "Take your choice. She or I will have to leave."

Lillian left her job and, becoming enamored of Dashiell Hammett at a meeting of the Writers Guild, she left her husband and the state of California. She achieved fame with her first play, *The Children's Hour*. Newspaper interviewers tossed brickbats at MGM for using her as a reader and ignoring her writing talents but no one told them that not even her husband considered her a writer at that time. In fact, no one told them that she had a husband at all.

When Lillian and I met again at the Goldwyn Studio, the cautious and watchful armistice between us held only until another rift occurred. Scenarist Virginia Kellogg was developing an idea called *Honeymoon in Reno*. Goldwyn had first refusal on it and provided her with an office next to Lillian's, who hadn't been seen at the studio for several days. I called to see if she was ill. She wasn't. As usual, she was backing a cause, this time a strike by the Motion Picture Scenic Artists.

When Goldwyn missed the presence of his author, he telephoned to see why she didn't come in.

"I don't cross picket lines," she told him.

Goldwyn accepted her stand cheerfully. "So work at home," he told her.

Finally, she missed the camaraderie of her pals and approached the strikers straggling about the studio's main gate.

She asked if they minded if she went inside. The picket leader shrugged and said, "Do anything you like, lady."

"Dope!" she shouted and crossed the line to work in her office. Then she noticed Virginia Kellogg in the room next door.

"Her typewriter is driving me crazy," she told Goldwyn. "It never stops. She can't be any good. How can she be a writer when she never takes a minute to think?"

I was consulted and said it wasn't unusual for writers to ponder their ideas at night and put them on paper the next day. But Goldwyn preferred Lillian's logic and terminated Kellogg's arrangement. It was the only time I knew a Hollywood writer to be dismissed for writing too much.

The month Goldwyn had predicted we would need to find his year's supply of stories dropped off the calendar and nothing was said about it. He referred to me only as his story editor. He had revealed an insensitive streak in many ways, heaping scorn and abuse on Hulburd and Haight that turned me away from reminding him of promises of a producership.

"You don't have to be a masochist to work here," said Kohlmar, "but it helps."

With relief, I heard Goldwyn agree I might have greater success with our quest for story material in New York.

It meant leaving Marie at home. After nine years in romantic places, with candlelight, soft music, and lovemaking, she had become pregnant at last. She was ecstatic, even when her doctor warned that in order to stay on a track to motherhood she would have to remain in bed. It was the first of two such lengthy periods that led to the birth of our two sons.

Immediately on arriving in New York I hit the jackpot, lunching at the "21" Club with Ernest Hemingway.

The bluff, heavy-set titan of American letters had just returned from Spain, where he had engaged in numerous actions of battle and bottle during the failed revolution. He was writing a novel laid in that background and told me just enough about the four days in the life of Robert Jordan to make me realize it was a movie prize. Best of all, Hemingway was willing to sell at once, for fifty thousand dollars, if Goldwyn could guarantee Gary Cooper as the star.

Excited, I telephoned Goldwyn from the restaurant, explained what a coup this was, praising Hemingway's writing and its best-seller qualities. He didn't see it that way at all.

How could I say it seemed a great role for Gary Cooper when I had never read the story? How could I even be sure Hemingway was writing such a book? I had not seen a single sheet of paper to prove it.

"You are trying to rob me," he said.

Before he hung up the phone, Goldwyn suggested I tell Hemingway to change the title.

"For Whom the Bell Tolls is like my story editor," he laughed, suddenly genial. "Makes no sense."

His cheerful reaction was just the opposite to mine, and neither was I cheered when friends at MGM reported to Marie that the movie I left behind had been previewed so successfully that further installments in the life of the Hardy Family were being developed. As I had left the scene, they would be produced by Carey Wilson.

I couldn't believe any finer prize than the Hemingway book was going to be found in New York. Discouraged by that, I told Goldwyn that if I failed to come up with anything he liked it would be another indication I was trying to rob him and I was returning to the studio. Whereupon, with another display of cheerfulness, he ordered me to stay in the East and find the best available writers.

"Find the people Irving Thalberg liked," he said, adding gaily, "so your trip shouldn't be a total loss."

That New York trip in the winter of 1937 did produce a total gain through the presence of Beatrice Kaufman, wife of George S. She accepted the job of eastern story editor and every moment around that bubbling, tawny-maned woman was a delight.

I went after former Thalberg devotees Anita Loos, Donald Ogden Stewart, and Laurence Stallings. Beatrice approached novelist Fannie Hurst, playwright Sidney Kingsley, and Dorothy Parker. Goldwyn expressed his enthusiasm for all of them. We should have known that he couldn't use them without increasing the number of productions, but Beatrice was already suffering from the same Goldwynesque malaise that I did, logic eluded us in our eagerness to effect some evidence of achievement.

While I was in New York, William Van Dusen, the public relations head of Pan-American Airways, suggested a movie about the pioneering of overseas flying. The airline was soon to start scheduled passenger flights between New York and Bermuda. Pan-Am was eager to find a Hollywood filmmaker to dramatize this. They offered Goldwyn "first refusal."

By refreshing his memory about early movie block-busters *The Covered Wagon* and *The Iron Horse,* and indicating to him that airplanes were an extension of trails and railroads, we won Goldwyn's approval for the idea. With that, Beatrice and I added another name to our list of wanted writers, Sidney Howard, the screen writer of *Gone With the Wind.* His completed scenario lay dormant while producer David Selznick sweated out how to get Clark Gable and find the right actress for the role of Scarlett O'Hara.

Howard was excited by the Pan-Am story, *Transatlantic Flight,* and Goldwyn agreed to let him take on the writing of the airline story even though it would be interrupted when *Gone With the Wind* required additional work from him.

My New York trip had taken on an aura of success. The city's wealth of talent gave Beatrice and me rich opportunities to search out people who would enhance Goldwyn's movies. She looked to Fannie Hurst to create a story that would star violinist Jascha Heifetz.

With *Transatlantic Flight* and the Heifetz film, Goldwyn had two stories in work for his 1938 program. A third was *The Goldwyn Follies,* planned as a collection of songs, dances, humorous skits, and beautiful "Goldwyn Girls." It was a cinematic clone of Broadway's celebrated *Ziegfeld Follies,* and he intended to make annual editions but was unable to decide who would write the first one.

Before returning to the studio, I partied with friends at a Greenwich Village nightclub. S. J. Perelman sat at the far end of our long table. I realized that a woman seated near him was leering at me in a peculiar way. I avoided her gaze but then Perelman passed a note down.

Sam: This woman on my left says you're a blend of Picasso and Harold Ross—She's mad for you.

Sid

Sacrificing my chances for the romance of the century, especially because it was obvious she was very drunk, I sent back the following:

Sid: Please tell her I write like Picasso and paint like Ross.

Sam

I returned to Hollywood to find Goldwyn almost totally involved with the *Follies.* He was so occupied that he informed me he didn't wish to be side-tracked by other projects. However, he was pleased to welcome visiting author Edna Ferber when I brought her into his office.

"What are you writing now?" he asked.

"My autobiography," she said.

"What's it about?"

She started to tell him, then stopped and laughed. With a bemused look, Goldwyn joined in.

In January 1937, the producer engaged George and Ira Gershwin to write the score for his film. Down the hall, choreographer George Balanchine, a shy young Russian, was selecting dances for a ballet of Gershwin's tone poem, *An American in Paris.*

But there were discordant notes in these harmonious proceedings. Goldwyn had no story for this planned opus, no script was being written. He thought Dorothy Parker and Alan Campbell could do it but they were in no hurry to take on the assignment and lingered in New York. Art Director Richard Day was refusing to renew his contract and Merritt Hulburd, plagued by headaches spawned by hypertension, wanted to return to the peace of Independence Square and the *Saturday Evening Post.*

I kept Beatrice informed about studio happenings. For reasons never explained to his staff, Goldwyn insisted he have a code name, Panama, in all interoffice memoranda, a curious subterfuge because the word appeared so often in all the company correspondence that the most obtuse decoder would have no trouble figuring out who Panama was meant to be.

Her reply carried a note, "Personal—Not for the files."

I had lunch with Sidney Kingsley the other day who told me in his own imitable halting fashion the story of his picture. It sounded quite good—melodramatic, exciting and colorful—but I cannot allow myself to be enthusiastic before I see something on paper. He's a terribly slow worker and why he should be doing all this for nothing is more than I can understand. He has some idiotic sense of gratitude towards Panama for buying Dead End. *I told him not to try to work the whole story out in too much detail, because I thought it would be much better if he let us see something so that those whiz-bang boys on the coast could get their little fat, greedy hands into it and tear it to pieces and re-build it before it was too late.*

I had Dotty and Alan pretty much in my power over the weekend because of the misbehavior of their nasty dog. They came over Friday night at 10:30 to hear the final verdict and when I first asked them for options, they said 'no.' At that moment their large black-and-white coach dog deposited one of the largest and moistest bowel movements I have ever seen in the middle of my pale grey living room rug. We had hardly settled down after this catastrophe when the dog playfully knocked a brimming full highball glass out of Alan's hand onto a beige chair . . . If I had played my cards

right, I could have gotten them for that original $1250,
I think.

My new office is exquisitely beautiful. I am glad I
shall not be there to hear Panama belly-aching when
he gets the bills. The color effect is tan, with white
leather chairs, Venetian blinds, and a casting couch.

Love to you, dear boy, and three cheers for Alma
Mater . . .

Beatrice

Despite Goldwyn saying he only had time for the *Follies,* I
coaxed him to consider a manuscript I brought back from New
York. By pointing out that the story was just right for his exotic
star Merle Oberon, I worked out details of its purchase with its
agent by phone after Goldwyn approved her price of twenty
thousand dollars. That new book was *We Are Not Alone* by
James Hilton, and reading it reminded me of a memorable
moment at MGM.

Kate Corbaley had fixed me with that schoolteacher look
that sixtyish ladies are able to summon at will, handed me a
copy of the *Atlantic Monthly* and said, "I don't know what you
plan doing with your next half hour, but you are going to stay
right where you are and read a great story."

That was *Goodbye, Mr. Chips,* about a shy and revered
teacher. It depicted the universal relationship scholars everywhere have shared with a beloved educator. We bought it for
six thousand dollars before Mrs. Corbaley's astute evaluation
was echoed by Alexander Woollcott, who trumpeted his discovery so vehemently the story of Mr. Chipping drew huge
sales in book form. At that price, its film rights proved to be a
great bargain.

That single opus catapulted James Hilton from literary ob-
scurity to world fame. Everything he wrote thereafter attracted
critical and movie studio attention.

Acquiring a Hilton story for Goldwyn was cause for celebration and the pleasant aura of achievement wasn't dampened even when, that same evening, I saw the sneak preview

of his newest film, produced by George Haight. *Woman Chases Man* was an excruciatingly unfunny comedy. The plot was stolen, as near as I could figure, from about fifty movies of the same genre. Even in the drab preview town of Huntington Park, a few miles outside the Hollywood area, where residents customarily sat resolutely still to get their money's worth of any toxic waste that studios dumped on them, they went home early that night. Goldwyn and Haight also fled quickly in a studio limousine.

I saw no connection between the previewed film and *We Are Not Alone*, but next morning Goldwyn sent for me and asked if I had bought the film rights to Hilton's book. I assured him I had, which he knew anyway because I wasn't authorized to do it without him.

Without a word of explanation, he telephoned the agent.

"My story editor is new here and made a mistake," he told her. "He was not supposed to do what he did and I should like you to forget what he told you." After further conversation, he closed the call with an exchange of felicitations and hung up, then smiled at me and said, "You see? She was happy to let me out of it when I explained."

Stunned with disbelief, I went back to empty my desk, knowing the only honorable thing to do was take my belongings and make for the nearest exit.

Freddy Kohlmar, my best friend on the lot, was waiting in the office with George Haight. "Take a deep breath and relax," grinned Freddy. "If you're wondering what hit you, George will explain."

Haight had no remorse for the role he played in dynamiting the purchase of Hilton's book.

"I had to ride back from the preview with the boss. It was the last thing I wanted him to think about, so I kicked dust in his eyes by knocking the story he just bought. When he steered our talk to *Woman Chases Man*, I opened fire on *We Are Not Alone*. Stick around and get even and some day you can give me the shaft."

I stayed on, but never forgave myself for doing so. Within

a week, *Variety* reported that Warner Brothers had acquired *We Are Not Alone*. It was apparent that the agreeable literary agent knew she had a back-up sale for the story.

All party spirit had left me but I wasn't alone, I was surrounded by fellow workers who felt the same way.

With the expiration of Richard Day's contract near, he avoided top-level meetings so new negotiations couldn't be initiated.

One day Goldwyn drifted in on Reeves Espy, his top business affairs officer, just before noon when Espy and Day were accustomed to lunching together. Goldwyn suggested he would join them. Uneasily, Espy said he would let him know but Goldwyn asked him to pick up the phone and arrange it at once.

Very gingerly, Espy did as directed, enunciating slowly into the phone, "Dick, Mr. Goldwyn would like to have lunch with us today—" Then with a furious burst of speed, "Dickhesstandingrightbesideme!"

Anita Loos was always a Thalberg favorite and Goldwyn approved the idea she should write a Gary Cooper comedy. She was currently freelancing. I brought her to Goldwyn's office where he offered her a two-year contract. Anita thought two years a long time and was disinclined to accept it but then he offered $5,000 a week for its full hundred-and-four-weeks. Practical lady that she was, she accepted.

Later, I told him I was pleased at his valuation of my friend's ability but couldn't see how, with his limited program, he could make effective use of her for two years at such high pay.

"Don't give it a thought, my boy," he said. "I have ways to finish contracts."

He was opening a peephole for me to see how I, too, might not work out my tour of duty but I didn't notice at the time. The point was even more noticeable shortly thereafter, when Anita completed her assignment and was sufficiently unhappy to toss away her contract and escape.

Meanwhile, I decided to do the best I could with life at

Goldwyn's, hoping to see the fun aspect of this period. There was plenty of laughs connected with the *Follies,* but not much else. *Transatlantic Flight* was grounded by the continuing postponements of *Gone with the Wind.*

Sidney Howard was researching the Pan-American story but mourned his problems with producer Selznick, who could, and did, summon him quite often.

From his farm at Tyringham, Massachusetts, Sidney wrote me that so much time had elapsed since he wrote the first draft of *Gone with the Wind,* he was "not now unnaturally completely cold." He added, regarding the screenplay that would win him the Academy Award, "Of course there is a possibility of a further postponement of *Gone with the Wind,* but even that will not help us materially. If I can get out of it, I can go to work at once on this Pan-American job, do a thorough piece of reporting and go right on to a treatment and a first draft all in one fell swoop and without interruption before the rehearsals of my play, and report to Hollywood for polishing up in November after the play has opened, and have the whole thing on ice in plenty of time. God damn *Gone with the Wind* . . ."

Goldwyn didn't mind that Sidney Howard was sidetracked. He was obsessed by the *Follies.* For all-round, day-by-day insanity, few movies are likely to come close to matching the madness that enveloped the making of that production.

In the tradition of show business revues, he wanted it to be all fun and music with some obligatory hint of young romance. To concoct that celluloidic mosaic, Goldwyn vacillated daily over writers. He transferred his desire for Dorothy Parker and Alan Campbell to George S. Kaufman. Beatrice wrote, "Panama phones him once a week and asks George to work on the *Follies* but he is panting at the bit to finish a new play and I don't think it would be possible to swerve him from this course."

With that, Goldwyn took aim at Parker and Campbell. He asked them to hurry their arrival to California. Beatrice wrote, "I told them that Panama wanted them to work on *Follies* and I am hoping this will be the case as I sold them on going a couple of weeks earlier than they wished because they thought it would be an amusing assignment." But by the time the team reached Hollywood, Goldwyn didn't want them.

A lanky, Philadelphian, Harry Kurnitz, had become his first choice. Kurnitz enjoyed considerable popularity in social gatherings. He brought his violin to the parties and was also adept with amusing one-liners. Like many wits, his sharp tongue could draw blood. He turned down a ride from Lillian Hellman in a newly imported German folk-waggen, saying, "I've been in bigger women than this."

It annoyed her and she registered a negative vote against him with Goldwyn. Kurnitz's career continued to thrive, although he viewed screen writing as an ordeal in which "Sadistic producers torture you beyond endurance by holding your jaws open while they drop gold dollars into your mouth in monotonously maddening succession."

Goldwyn finally decided on the screen writer for the film— the ever-available, endlessly imaginative and colorful Ben Hecht. It would be his task to concoct the sequences that would tie together the songs, dances, and witty sayings.

Hecht went about it with his usual regard for moviemaking shenanigans. He demanded and received a dimly lit office suite with a beautiful Goldwyn dancing girl in a beaded evening dress as a receptionist outside his office. He broadcast a call through the studio for eighteen baseball players to meet daily for a post-luncheon game, an effort that failed when less than six would-be athletes responded. Thereupon, he called for bridge players and an ongoing tournament occupied his afternoons.

Goldwyn accepted Hecht's doings with a philosophical hope that the presence of paper and pencil for keeping the bridge score might trigger usable notions to incorporate in the movie. The game also anchored Ben to his office, the contest ending each afternoon with the arrival of the company accountant with one thousand dollars in cash which the writer demanded for his services.

Information about casting changes in the proposed film

reached Hecht like wartime dispatches, all of which he accepted with stoic indifference. He never argued with the changes thrown at him, blithely accepted them all and renewed every discarded sequence with an instant replacement.

Moviemaking was a new milieu for George Balanchine and he sought advice on how to go about it from all his new friends in the studio. Universally he was warned not to divulge his choreography of *American in Paris* to Goldwyn until it was blocked out and ready. Thereupon, the stage he worked on was securely locked and a guard stationed at the door. But Goldwyn felt deprived and one day he accosted Balanchine with the outright demand that as boss, he be allowed to see the work in progress. Cornered, Balanchine tried to evade the audition.

"Let me explain in my own way, Mr. Goldwyn," he said. "I ask you to visualize the tempo, the artistry of the dance, the blinding colors that will dazzle your eyes when I call on you to see it. But for now, let me put it this way . . . "

He put his hands close together and snapped his fingers.

"That is the first movement, it is what I call Major."

He moved his hands to the left of his body, snapping his fingers again and said, "This is what I call Minor." He swung his hands in rapidly increasing cadence, alternating each snap of the fingers, "Major! Minor! Major! Minor!" and might have gone on indefinitely but a beaming Goldwyn broke in, "I like it!"

When Balanchine finally opened the stage door for Goldwyn to see his concept of *An American in Paris*, the producer rejected it. He demanded different music and a different dance be substituted. But the music would not be by George Gershwin.

While working on the score for *The Goldwyn Follies*, the composer began to complain of a persistent headache and a strange odor of burning rubber that nobody else could detect.

He had performed as soloist with the Los Angeles Philharmonic Orchestra on February 11 playing his *Concerto in F*.

Marie and I were there, and also attended a party for the composer at the Trocadero, a Hollywood nightclub.

When George arrived, Oscar Levant looked accusingly at him. That gifted pianist was as expert as George himself at interpreting his compositions. George, in turn, had no problem interpreting Levant's look. He grinned and said, "I thought of you when I did it, you bastard."

But Levant had recognized that Gershwin slurred a passage while playing one of his own compositions in public, something quite unheard of (in a true sense of that overused phrase).

As the headaches continued to plague him, George went to a doctor for a physical check-up and was told everything was fine. He continued writing music for the *Follies* with his brother Ira in an office just beneath mine, and the sounds of a song they would call "Love Walked In" were hammered out with continuing stops and starts, as both lyric and melody took final shape. Then, one day, the music stopped. A new medical evaluation contained a much gloomier diagnosis.

Ira Gershwin phoned Goldwyn to say that his brother was going into a hospital for further examinations and when he hung up, Goldwyn took them off the payroll.

On July 11, Gershwin died while undergoing an operation for a brain tumor. The unfinished score and music for a new ballet was completed by Vernon Duke.

Gershwin's death devastated the Goldwyn staff. Merritt Hulburd, oppressed by massive headaches of his own, decided to return to the *Saturday Evening Post*, which appeared to offer a panacea for the ailments of mind and body that tormented his Hollywood career.

The day he departed, Goldwyn opened his private dining room for a luncheon honoring the staff member who was going over the wall. During it, Goldwyn promised we might all count on a similar luncheon on leaving the firm. But the producer was speechless when Hulburd asked, "Can they use the room to give you a lunch when *you* leave, Mr. Goldwyn?"

Negotiations for Fannie Hurst to come west and write an original story for Jascha Heifetz bogged down, and when Beatrice Kaufman couldn't resolve the impasse, I received this mournful letter from the author.

Dear Sammarx:
What are we going to do!
Our lawyers can't seem to get together. We naturally feel within our rights and you feel within yours, and the deadlock goes on and on. It will be horrid if Mr. Goldwyn returns to unsigned contracts, especially since I have written my story practically in its entirety.
Isn't there something we as innocent bystanders can do to accelerate matters? I agree with my lawyer's point of view, and yet I want to do a Goldwyn picture.
I hope you had a good holiday and have brought back a rested and bang-up point of view that will solve our tired dilemma.

Fannie Hurst

But I had no better luck than Beatrice, who had turned her back on studio problems and was vacationing at Neshobe Island, Vermont, where party spirits prevailed. Her letters continued to highlight the fun.

Dear Sam:
Your letter arrived this morning and gave me great pleasure and amusement, too. I could not resist reading a couple of the Panama lines to the boys and Alice Duer Miller and they roared with pleasure. High-spotted, as your correspondence is, it makes life chez Goldwyn sound highly entertaining.
Here it is almost a continual riot. Harpo rises with the sun, thumbs his harp which he has had sent up here at great expense and bother, and swishes the strings until we all appear.

We play croquet with enormous venom for hours, swim, play badminton, hearts, cribbage and bridge until midnight. Harp's energy is fantastic; he is like a tempest which never loses its vitality for a moment. Yesterday, in a quiet moment, he started to read the Bible. "There isn't any character you can root for," he complained after a few minutes. Pause. Then: "This guy don't know how to write. He doesn't even introduce his characters!" I suppose he is the only primitive person left in the whole world.

Dr. Gustav Eckstein, the bird man, has just left. A quiet little fellow with a soprano voice, white skin, and infinite charm. Retiring, a vegetarian, and very simple. Whenever there was a lull in conversation he told us about his canaries. Have you ever read any of his books? They are quite swell . . . Jo Alsop is here—a young Groton-Harvard youth, cousin to the Roosevelts (and practically everyone else in the world) who is Washington correspondent on the Tribune. He used to be a mass of a fellow, encased in numberless cushions of fat. He has been at Johns-Hopkins for three months and worked off sixty-five pounds. Awfully smart, if a little precious. And the Guinzburgs, Alice M. and George.

Woollcott is going over to have dinner with Dorothy Thompson tomorrow—they have a house about forty miles from here and I thought of going along to clinch the Sinclair Lewis novel, but Alex says he is not there. He is supposed to be in Europe, and one hears they have definitely busted. I spoke to his agent Anne Watkins before I left about it; she swears that we will get it immediately, but I have learned to distrust all agents of all sexes.

More later; this is getting dull.

It's two days later now, Alex went to Dorothy Thompson's last night for dinner. Lewis is living in Stockbridge (perhaps at Dr. Riggs Sanitarium?) but showed up unexpectedly at dinner time. They have not separated, however, and Dorothy went to some lengths to make this clear. The book's title is Prodigal Parents,

about parents sick and sore at their children's going on—po-
litically, morally and aesthetically. Publication date January.
He told Alex it was finished.

The August theatrical prospects are horrible; there is noth-
ing that sounds like even palatable fare except the Stallings
musical which opens the very end of the month. Nor does
September look much more promising.

I'd love to change spots with you for a while. Why don't
you see if you can wangle it for November; that's a good
month for you because the shows are mostly in by then. Or
any time that you want; it doesn't matter to me.

Harp has ordered the latest Marx Brothers picture for us in
a local town for Friday. They had already had it, but hurried it
back when he promised a personal appearance.

Enough of this rambling. I'm off to Woodstock to lunch,
and then to see the Orozco paintings in the library at Dartmouth.
I may enroll for graduate work. Or shall I continue ignorant
and occasionally happy as Panama's NY spy?

Love to you dear boy, and how is that pretty little girl?
Beatrice

Finally the filming of the *Goldwyn Follies* was completed and
in the editing room.

Goldwyn elected to take a vacation in Hawaii. With his
chauffeured limousine waiting outside with wife and luggage,
he summoned the staff to his office. We stood in a line against
the wall as he delivered a pep talk about working hard in his
absence. Then, very gravely, he circled the room, shook
everybody's hands and wished each of us "Bon Voyage."

On his return, *Goldwyn Follies* was previewed to a
Huntington Park audience. The reaction was a far cry from the
homage Goldwyn hoped to reap from it. Most of the scenes
were greeted by a lack of enthusiasm bordering on sheer ap-
athy. Only one sequence with one artist electrified the theatre
occupants. It was a great surprise to the producer, coming as
it did for a ventriloquist that Kohlmar had signed up.

Goldwyn hurriedly assembled his staff on the curb outside the theatre, very much like the huddle of a football team, and whispered the strategy for the next play. "Nobody tell that fellow with his dummy how good he is until I make a new deal with him."

It was apparent that our boss was the last person in America who didn't know that during the year *Follies* was in preparation, Edgar Bergen and Charley McCarthy had achieved national popularity through weekly radio appearances.

Solemnly, there on the pavement outside the preview theatre, we swore to keep the secret the boss demanded of us.

After Hulburd departed, George Haight fell into disfavor. He refused to cancel the remaining months of his contract, whereupon Goldwyn demoted him from associate producer to story analyst and moved him into a closetlike receptacle, where he worked out his remaining contract time writing synopses.

The staff might well reflect, then, that their boss knew what he was doing when he wished everyone "Bon Voyage" the day he sailed for Hawaii.

Russia and Finland were at war and Goldwyn headed up a Finnish relief fund. Zealously dedicated to that purpose, he spent hours on the phone seeking financial help for the small, beleaguered and distant land.

In the midst of his campaign for Finland he called me to his office. "You're not happy here, are you?" he said.

I was floored by the abruptness with which he was opening the way to freedom.

"You're right," I said. "I'm definitely unhappy."

"Would you like to leave?" he asked.

Would I? Before I could offer a fervent assent, he took an incoming phone call.

The caller thought Finland was a goner any time the Russian bear snapped its military fangs. He questioned if the money he would donate could be safely delivered to Finland before it surrendered.

"I personally guarantee that Finland will not surrender," Goldwyn shouted into the phone. Somehow satisfying his caller that he was in command of the situation, he was promised a donation. He was a happy man when he hung up the phone and I told him I was willing to abrogate our employment deal that very hour. He shook my hand with a warmth that hadn't passed between us since our first meeting. I wished him a sardonic "Bon Voyage" for which he thanked me.

Through those Hollywood years, I had seen Harry Cohn at numerous affairs; he always invited me to tell him if I wanted a job. The head of Columbia Pictures Studio was cut from a different mold than Goldwyn. Goldwyn presented a facade of snobbishness that he projected like a trademark. He never used profanity, whereas Cohn peppered his conversations with obscenities. Cohn made no pretense of caring what others thought about him, he enjoyed being offensive and couldn't care less about his image, if he thought about it at all.

Even knowing those characteristics, I elected to call and say I was on the open market.

"Get your ass over here Monday morning," he commanded. "After Sam Goldwyn, Columbia will be like the Garden of Eden."

The Garden of Eden it wasn't, but Columbia rounded out the last months of the gaudy spree with fun and festivities.

Chapter Thirteen

$\boxed{\text{F}}$ eisty and balding Harry Cohn was an instinctive showman, a shrewd administrator, and, when one made an effort to understand his actions, oddly likeable. He could be petty and prejudiced or unexpectedly sympathetic. One of the statistical facts that he never disputed was that his enemies outnumbered his friends ten to one. He claimed that was how he wanted it, a defense mechanism to disguise his inability to win affection.

His office was directly over the entrance to the block-long studio on Gower Street, just off Sunset Boulevard. It had a picture window through which he watched everybody approaching his studio, his eyes darting streetward even in the midst of important conferences. The door to his private office was electronically sealed; no one could come in without his pushing the button that opened it. By watching visitors approach the front door, he knew who wanted to see him before they could get to the information desk below. He often gave the signal to the uniformed policeman, granting or forbidding entrance before the newcomer gave his name.

He was a manic gambler. His best friends were card sharks and bookmakers and when his office door was most securely locked, it was just as likely that a gin game was going on as a story conference.

Few writers ever had a nice word for Cohn. It was a literary standoff; he rarely had a nice word for writers.

He read all scripts from the viewpoint of uneducated Joe Schmuck whom he claimed was the average moviegoer. He wielded a large black editing pencil like an executioner's sword on stories and screenplays, his marginal objections might just as well have been dipped in blood. Story points, character touches, and dialogue he didn't understand were ruthlessly guillotined. He rejected any appeals from writers, no matter how anguished, judging all criticism as personal attacks on his own intelligence.

He struck out words like "tycoon" because his favorite fictitious filmgoer would think it was a "big wind." Audiences never met up with a character in a Columbia picture named Peter because, in Harry Cohn's world, Peter signified male genitals.

In reality, he was the man he claimed was fictitious. Sometimes a whole scene was circled in black with "Don't get it" or "What the hell does this mean?" in the margin. They were messages from Harry Cohn, not Joe Schmuck. Sometimes an explanation from the author might win a reprieve, but if Cohn's marking was a capitalized NO, then no argument could save it.

The general standard of Columbia's feature films ranged from awful to abysmal but the law of averages worked in its favor and each year a couple of films emerged that compared favorably with those made anywhere.

In the beginning, they came mainly from a director Cohn held in awe, whose scripts he dared not change, whose talents he was wise enough to recognize and respect.

As Columbia grew in stature, Cohn could thank Frank Capra for the education that brought it about. Without Capra, Columbia might never have survived the silent era, but survive it did and it was a thriving organization when Cohn invited me into it. By then he had two other directors of ability available to him, Howard Hawks and Gregory La Cava.

Well-informed friends described my new boss as a clown, a mountebank, a crook, a fool, and a killer. They supplied convincing evidence to warrant such accusations. But until he performed some evil action against me, I decided to withhold my opinion and I'm glad I did.

Louis B. Mayer impressed me. Goldwyn intimidated me. Cohn did neither. But as an outgoing personality, he over-shadowed both of them. He was amusing and entertaining, he was devious but he didn't try to hide it. He possessed money, power, and influence, befitting any movie studio head, but he couldn't acquire the importance of Mayer or Goldwyn and that hurt him deeply. I accepted his hilarious antics seriously enough to get along with him just fine. One didn't need even a rudimentary knowledge of psychology to see that he desperately wanted to be loved but was embarrassd by it and didn't know how to go about it.

Darryl Zanuck, head of production at 20th Century-Fox, enjoyed polo and when not out on the field he would brandish a mallet during story conferences. Because he played the game, no one thought much about it. At Columbia, Cohn whipped a polo mallet around, swiping at an imaginary ball on the floor and following its supposed flight directly between goal posts that weren't there. When he wasn't winning at polo, Cohn carried a riding whip in his hand; it accompanied him when he sallied forth on studio stages and even into the private dining room where he had his lunch. However, nobody ever saw him on a horse.

About a month after I came to Columbia, Cohn asked Edgar Selwyn and me to lunch privately in his office. He wanted to discuss a very personal situation.

As an example of naiveté gone rampant, he confided to us a real-life incident he believed had elements worthy of drama-tization. His question was whether he should make a movie of it or hire a playwright to put it on the stage. He wanted Selwyn, a former Broadway producer, to make the decision.

This was the story:

Cohn and his wife Rose were childless after many years of marriage. He had no heir to inherit his growing fortune. Visits to doctors indicated his wife was unable to have a child. Medical science could do nothing about it and neither could she.

One day, a writer suggested a film based on the love of Napoleon and Josephine and urged the making of a movie in which the Emperor fathered a child outside matrimony. Cohn was fascinated. At dinner with his wife, he told her how Napoleon handled this delicate situation. He assumed that she saw the similarity to their own problem and when she offered no objections to his hint that the same action would solve it for them, he took it to mean she approved.

Next day, he dropped in on a ballroom set and surveyed the extras. A well-built young female caught his eye. He told the assistant director to send her to his office when the company broke for lunch.

She came in, happily surprised, probably thinking she was about to be tapped for an important role in a film. The dialogue, however, didn't follow the conventional theme.

"Are you married?"

"No."

"Where do you live?"

"With my mother."

"Is there any reason you can't have a baby?"

When she recovered from her surprise, he went on.

"I want you to have one with me. I'll rent an apartment. If it's a boy you get fifty thousand dollars, if it's a girl, twenty-five. I keep the child. What do you say?"

"I don't know what to say."

"Well, go home and tell your mother and let me know what she says."

Romance it wasn't.

Next day, they drew up an agreement and all three of them signed it and in a matter of weeks she told him she was pregnant.

He conveyed the news of his impending fatherhood to his wife Rose, who was sitting across the dining room table from him when he broke the happy tidings. It required some adroit ducking to avoid the tableware she threw at him. She claimed to have no recollection of his conversation about Napoleon and Josephine and even if he had meant it to have special meanings between them, it didn't excuse his actions.

"There's more to this than just screwing some innocent kid," she said. They left their dinner and drove to the home of Mendel Silberberg, the company lawyer.

"Tell him what you've done," she commanded her now-deflated husband.

"You just lost your studio, Harry," said the lawyer. "You're trafficking in a human soul and it was idiotic to sign a paper to prove it. She has evidence enough to come out of court with everything you own in the world."

The three of them drove pell-mell to the girl's apartment. For fifty thousand dollars, the girl agreed to destroy their contract and have an abortion.

I had been at Columbia less than a month when Cohn told this story. He told it like it was a Shakespearean tragedy. Selwyn asked time to think it over and, thankfully, the matter never came up again. A divorce between Rose and Harry Cohn loomed even closer and probably helped him decide the episode would better remain secret.

A few weeks after the occurrence passed into history, a studio publicity man resigned. Cohn didn't want to lose him and called him to his office to ask that he stay. But the publicity man refused, having completed plans for a honeymoon trip around the world. He told Cohn that his bride-to-be, a young film extra, had suddenly inherited fifty thousand dollars from an uncle in Australia.

As my relationship to Cohn grew close and friendly, I was running into the opposite from his studio manager. A former bookkeeper elevated to executive status, Samuel Briskin was second in command. When I joined the company, he showed his displeasure and made no secret of it. Cohn was amused. Interoffice feuds were a way of life at Columbia. He believed they made for stronger efforts of achievement, and as if to prove his point, he was at dagger-point with his brother Jack, his partner, kingpin of the New York office. Jack Cohn rarely came west; when he did, he not only never socialized with brother Harry, he rarely spoke to him.

Columbia was a studio of unbrotherly love in many ways. Sam Briskin's brother Irving ran a unit producing the low-budget films that were spewed forth as part of the company's program, to supply a complete show to theatres. As a producer of undistinguished movies lacking meritorious elements of any kind, Irving Briskin was without a peer. Sam Briskin tried to ignore the relationship.

There were other brother teams that didn't work together at Columbia. Writer Robert Riskin collaborated on scripts with director Capra, his brother Everett held a producing berth that delivered an uneven program, mixing good with the bad. Writer Sidney Buchman also produced films, usually of a high grade, while his writing brother Harold labored mostly in the Irving Briskin unit.

Intellectually, Sidney Buchman rated high with Cohn, who assigned him to the remake of a European film that depicted the life of Chopin. Since Cornel Wilde, who was to star in the role of the famed composer, could only simulate piano playing, he would be photographed at a soundless instrument and the music would be dubbed. A top caliber pianist was required to supply the musical tracks and, as it happened, Vladimir Horowitz, the most ideal of all candidates, was about to give a concert in Los Angeles.

The Horowitz performance was on a Friday night, the night of the week when Cohn went regularly to the Hollywood Legion Stadium to view the boxing matches. He hated to miss them. It took persuasive pleas from Sidney Buchman to get him to go see the high-priced virtuoso. Buchman's pleadings that it was important to the movie won the day and Cohn agreed to attend the Horowitz concert.

In his seat down front on the keyboard side, Cohn seemed to be watching in a trance, eyes glued to the pianist's flying fingers.

During a momentary pause, Buchman asked, "How do you like him?"

"He's got a terrific left!" said the boxing devotee. Instead of Horowitz, a local virtuoso, Bernard Gimpel, was engaged to record the musical tracks for *A Song to Remember.*

Although Cohn was using me chiefly as his story editor, he did approve my producing a low-budget film, based on a complete screenplay by my friend Tess Slesinger.

It was a delicate story called *The Answer on the Magnolia Tree*, an atmospheric drama set at a girls' school, centering around the spring dance. It was an unusual film for Columbia, where blood and guts were considered the most attractive elements any film could have. Cohn assigned a newly arrived German director, John Brahm, to the film. Then he wished us both luck and departed to spend August at the races at Saratoga, taking along his favorite bookmaker, whose selections were expected to give Cohn permanent residence in the winners' circle.

My film, its title changed to *Girls School*, was now under the supervision of Sam Briskin, who proceeded to mangle every phase of it. He demanded a rewrite of the script, adding a villainous young woman to give the story "guts." He insisted on approving the casting of every young actress, two of whom would be needed for the leading roles.

As always, Hollywood was a happy hunting ground for aspiring young girls, and that summer of 1938 many destined to become stars were just starting their careers. Briskin summarily turned away everyone Brahm and I brought him, among them Lana Turner, Joan Fontaine, Yvonne De Carlo and Rita Hayworth, a pretty redheaded dancer who had a Columbia contract but was only in his brother Irving's movies. Ignoring any opinion from me or Brahm, he signed Nan Grey and Ann Shirley, both quite lovely and competent although neither ever approached the heights of stardom achieved by those he rejected.

When Cohn returned from Saratoga, I reported I had my fill of producing for him and would confine my activities to the peace and calm of the story department.

He was in a curiously apathetic mood and offered no objections. His hopes of huge winnings at Saratoga had gone astray. He suffered monumental losses despite the expertise of his bookmaker associate. On the day he returned to the studio, Cohn fired the bookmaker's son much to the young man's surprise as he had been hired on as a producer only a month before, also much to his surprise.

Through the 1930s, Herman Mankiewicz ambled in and out of the Hollywood studios, prolific as any screen writer could hope to be. He wrote and produced twelve feature films between 1930 and 1932, all at Paramount. He came to MGM and wrote eight films in the next two years. Wherever he was, his not-inconsiderable weight was felt. He had the body of a pugilist, a disarming grin, and the soul of a Voltaire. In his lifetime he would write seventy-five produced screenplays, but of the countless folk he created, he was truly his own best character.

In 1938, he was encountering hard times, mixing frank opinions and alcohol. Studio portals that once opened easily before him were slammed closed. Harry Cohn was one of the studio moguls who had developed an antagonism and refused to use him.

Columbia producer William Perlberg agreed with me that Mankiewicz was well-suited to adapt a domestic comedy on his slate, and we called on Cohn to hire him. Cohn did so, but reluctantly, and with such misgivings that the producer and I implored the writer to steer clear of the imperious boss. Other Mankiewicz friends, including Sidney Buchman, joined us. We needed all the help we could get because just telling Mankiewicz what not to do was like daring him to do it. He was asked to avoid Cohn, the front office, and adjacent hallways. The executive area was off-limits and, most important of all, he was implored to stay out of the small private dining room Columbia operated for its executives, writers, and directors. Cohn dominated all the actions and conversations in that small chamber.

The oblong table that filled the room had places for a dozen chairs. A thirteenth stood against a wall, fashioned exactly like the others but reserved for special guests. On occasion, Cohn would phone ahead and have it placed close to him at the head of the table. That chair was wired. Its dry batteries were activated by the weight of a human body sitting on it. It sent a pulsating throb through the derriere, accompanied by a deep and frightening buzz.

Unsuspecting newcomers had no inkling of the ordeal served them before the first course and usually leaped skyward with an appropriate yelp, to the merriment of Cohn and his regulars.

No outsider was ever respected so highly as to escape that tomfoolery. However, soon after I arrived, playwright Zoe Akins, a lady of extremely solid girth and many layers of skirts, failed to hear the buzz or feel the throb. She wore out the batteries before the nonplussed Cohn could persuade her she was sitting in an electric chair.

It was inevitable that Herman Mankiewicz could see no reason not to lunch in the private dining room. He laughed at his producer's fears. In Mank's lexicon, there was no such word as fear. Fear was reserved for the hearts of his admirers.

During the first few days of his writing assignment, Mankiewicz gladdened these hearts by absenting himself from the dining room. But then he showed up. Fortunately, Cohn did not. Mankiewicz delivered a few unchallenged comments on the state of the movie business, good-naturedly saying that if any of his listeners detected anything profound in his statements, he'd claim he was misquoted.

Emboldened by the success of his first visit, he began to lunch there regularly. And then it happened. He was at lunch there when Cohn walked in.

The studio boss embarked immediately on a critique of a new Lubitsch film, *Bluebeard's Eighth Wife*, which he had screened in his home the previous evening. When he predicted a huge flop for the great German comedy director, Mankiewicz stared at Cohn.

Sidney Buchman, sitting beside him, whispered, "Don't say what you're thinking, Herman!"

It was a futile warning. With exaggerated politeness, Mankiewicz said, "I'm truly amazed at your perceptiveness, Mr. Cohn. You have some special gift that permits you to know that this film will fail before it's even opened in a single theatre."

"You bet your ass I know," snapped Cohn. "When I sit still, it's a hit. When I'm antsy . . . " He illustrated by shifting about in his chair, ". . . like I was last night, it's a sure flop."

"In other words," said Mankiewicz, "you have a monitor ass wired to a hundred million other asses."

It was a pronouncement that would be quoted throughout Hollywood history. But Mankiewicz didn't stop there.

"You know, Mr. Cohn, every Lubitsch picture turns away thousands opening day at the Rivoli Theatre in New York."

"Except that the Rivoli doesn't hold thousands," said Cohn.

With that, Mankiewicz assumed the attitude of a sympathetic teacher dealing with a retarded child.

"The number of people turned away has nothing to do with what a theatre holds, Mr. Cohn. You can turn away a hundred thousand from the Rivoli. You can turn away a million from the Yankee Stadium. You can even turn away a hundred million from the Sistine Chapel!"

The luncheon audience enjoyed the show but word came later that day from Cohn to remove Mankiewicz from the payroll.

The purchase of film rights to the Broadway play *Golden Boy* prompted Cohn to send me to New York in search of a screen writer.

My first target was the young actor turned playwright, Clifford Odets. We met in his Greenwich Village apartment and set out for lunch.

"My treat," he said, and opened the top drawer of a large metal file that stood in his front room. From a section indexed with M, he drew out some money and we headed to a local delicatessen. There, he turned down my offer, using an excuse I was beginning to hear from many aspiring playwrights, a preference for the stage over the screen. Frank to a point as disarming as it was honest, Odets admitted that Hollywood filmmaking had its allure in many directions and some day in the future he would welcome a chance to make movies. But theatre came first.

My second choice was the Spewacks, the highly successful husband-and-wife collaborators I knew well. Short, bouncy Bella Spewack was the lively member of the team. She handled its business end while husband Sam would saunter behind, tall and lanky, seemingly disinterested in any plans she set up for them. In line with this indifference, he was also inclined to be absent-minded.

They were our house guests on past visits to California, where Marie had to cope with an odd habit. She had cigarette lighters about the house and Sam Spewack used them to light his pipe. Then he would absently put the lighter in his pocket. Apparently, while visiting the homes of other friends, he would fish it out, use it, and then assume it belonged there, so he would set it down and that was the last Marie ever saw of it. However, she reported that she lost some and won some. Sam also picked up lighters in the homes of friends, pocketed them and then set them down in our parlor.

The Spewacks also rejected my offer that they adapt *Golden Boy*. They had a new musical play, *Leave It to Me*, on Broadway after a Boston tryout. It was a hit, and in it, coy young Mary Martin stopped the show nightly with a Cole Porter song "My Heart Belongs to Daddy." They wanted to rest on their laurels and royalties.

However, Bella came to the Columbia office to ask a favor. She explained that also in Boston that week was another tryout, *Generals Die in Bed*, by a new playwright, Lewis Meltzer. Despite the popularity of its star, Ina Claire, the show failed. The New York run was cancelled.

Just before the play closed, Bella went to the Boston theatre and asked to see the author. The manager walked her out front and pointed to a lone figure seated on the commons. He was weeping.

"That's him," he said.

"I tried to cheer him up," she said. "But it wasn't easy. His dreams are dead. He's back in town now with all his future behind him. Look, give him a call, tell him you're looking for a writer for *Golden Boy* and you'd like to interview him. That's all I ask. Just let him know someone thought about him. I don't expect you to take him."

Meltzer had been with the Group Theatre, the same small Depression outfit in which Odets started his career. He came to the office fired up with thoughts of how *Golden Boy* could be filmed, and when director Rouben Mamoulian arrived in New York to meet the writer possibilities I lined up for him, he wanted Meltzer above all others. He also selected Daniel Taradash and both became favorites of Harry Cohn, remaining on the studio staff for years.

Not long after this, Clifford Odets showed up at the studio in Hollywood, coming straight from the train. He wanted to discuss something very personal, and we agreed to do so that evening. Meanwhile, I sent him to our house in Beverly Hills. Marie was out, so I alerted the maid to let him in.

He was upstairs when Marie arrived. She met him for the first time as he stepped nude out of the shower just as she walked in. It would have made an interesting sequence in any movie, particularly as she had no idea who he was.

Later that evening, he disclosed the personal matter that brought him west. He wanted an introduction to Luise Rainer. "I'm going to marry her," he said.

It was arranged next day and soon afterward, they married. Also soon afterward, they divorced. As he explained it, he had found it difficult to keep up with her changes of mind.

"We had one conversation during which she told me how much she loved Hollywood and would spend the rest of her life there. A few minutes later, she said New York was the only place for her and she would take the next train. A few minutes later she wished she was in Europe and we should have a baby. I told her she couldn't do all those things in one night and that finished the marriage."

Cohn constantly excused questionable actions by claiming he had to be practical and keep the best interests of his company uppermost. That was his rationale when I protested an outrageous trick perpetrated on Grace Moore.

A lovely prima donna, Grace had a down-up-down movie career. She failed miserably in early picturizations at MGM, then starred in a fabulous hit, *One Night of Love*, at Columbia. But her subsequent efforts lacked box office luster.

One more movie was owed on her Columbia contract. Cohn had no plans for it. He hoped the singer would elect to forego further movie-making, encouraged by statements she made on a concert tour that film might not be her metier. But then, "out of a blue sky," as he put it, she telegraphed him she was arriving in Hollywood and would be on hand when the contractual date for that production arrived.

In other studios, or so it seemed to me, there were two options. They could cancel their efforts to produce a film and pay off their obligation to the star or they would make an effort to do a worthwhile picture and stand to win or lose in an industry that was based on such gambles. But Cohn chose a third option, taking a calculated risk, trusting to his shrewd instincts that it would get the desired result without cost to the studio.

He telegraphed the star that he had a superb script ready for her and her producer would be waiting to hand it to her when her train arrived in Los Angeles.

The producer had never produced a film. Joseph Sistrom was a devoted assistant to director Frank Capra. Sartorially he left much to be desired. His unkempt hair hung over his shoulders, he shlepped around in unpressed garments and sandals. He had an inordinant fondness for beer and rarely was seen without a can of it in his hand.

Withal, he was ambitious and intellectual. He had long

sought a producing berth with Cohn and was thrilled by the prospect he could make a picture with Grace Moore. Even the script that Cohn handed him failed to deter his enthusiasm, although it was to be a remake of an Irving Briskin western story. He would be allowed only to change a few lines and add a few songs. Nevertheless, he readily accepted the assignment and was waiting dutifully at the Santa Fe Station when his star arrived on the arm of a new, handsome husband.

Some two hours after Sistrom left her at her hotel, the star telephoned Cohn and refused to make the picture, cancelling the contract. It worked out just as he expected. On such tactics, Cohn achieved his reputation as a killer.

By virtue of film biographies suggested to him, he saw himself as Napoleon the conqueror; Nero the Emperor wielding the power of life and death over all his people; Alexander the Great of Macedonia, ruler of the earth; and Solomon of Israel, a man of fabulous wealth and wisdom. Inside the walled-in world of Columbia Studios, Cohn was indeed all of these.

He felt these beliefs were justified, if one ruled over a film studio. Movie-making required more than imagination and inventiveness, which were for writers and directors. The man at the top had to mix showmanship with ruthlessness and Cohn felt he knew how to do it. And he had to have more. He had to have luck and the intelligence to exploit it to the fullest. Cohn felt he had these, too. He had a situation he could use as an example.

Like the contract with Grace Moore, there was an obligation to make a film with Cary Grant. Unlike Miss Moore, Grant was a desirable star and failure to make the contractual movie would be a solid loss to the company. Just as desperation closed in on him, director Howard Hawks showed up with writer Jules Furthman.

Their appearance was so fortunate, so miraculously accidental, that whether Cohn was lucky or not, it could be likened to a fire engine just happening by a building enveloped in flames.

They offered an original story, a salty saga of renegade fliers in the lush tropics of Central America. That Hawks could have known Columbia had an obligation to make a film with Grant and no story to go with it probably occurred to Cohn, but it hardly mattered. What was important was that Hawks and Furthman were prepared to start their production immediately. All they needed was a simulated runway amid palm trees and they would make up the scenes as they went along. On that premise, the filming of *Only Angels Have Wings* began.

The highly creative skills of Hawks as a director were well-matched by the screen-writing ability of Jules Furthman, who was blessed with a superb memory and the mental agility to recycle stories to fit any situation. He wrote the exciting sequence in Thalberg's *China Seas* in which a huge locomotive tears loose on the deck of a freighter in a storm, careening back and forth like an uncaged dinosaur. Reminded that his behemoth exactly resembled Victor Hugo's *Old One Hundred* and that the great French author's classic depiction of a rampaging cannon had to be his inspiration, Furthman shrugged and said, "If you use another writer's idea precisely, that's plagiarism; when you use it imprecisely, that's research!"

Only Angels Have Wings was an instant hit.

It was seen by millions, but possibly few who witnessed this entertaining melodrama gave it the close attention that Sam Briskin did. Cohn's studio manager had left him to take up the reins at RKO, a neighboring studio barely a stone's throw down Gower Street. He called Cohn for an appointment. He was going to throw a huge stone at his former boss.

Along with members of his legal department, Briskin brought along a year-old RKO film, *Five Came Back*. It was screened in the projection room that adjoined Cohn's office. No explanation was made, no questions were asked and there was no need for conversation while the film unspooled. The plot of the little program picture was the obvious source of *Only Angels Have Wings*.

When the movie ended and the lights came on in the projection room, Briskin basked in a glow of smug triumph.

"Just pay us the profits from *Only Angels Have Wings* and we don't sue."

"Thank you for the show," said Cohn. "I'll see you in court."

"As two old friends, I don't want to call you a thief," said Briskin. "You can settle out of court and save yourself the humiliation and the extra costs."

"I'd rather do it my way," said Cohn. "I'll just buy stock in RKO so I can be at the next stockholder meeting. I want to see your face when you're asked why you failed to recognize a great story when you had it and made it into a shitty B-picture. I may be the one who'll ask, so I can say I saw that you had bungled the job and decided to show the public the right way to handle it. I don't think you'll be running the studio much longer, Sam."

Briskin and his legal group took the print of their picture back and nothing more was heard from them. Jules Furthman shrugged when Cohn accused him of stealing from the RKO film. "All the good stories have been told," said the writer. "It's how you tell them that makes the difference between the old and the new."

The next film Hawks and Furthman made for Cohn also starred Cary Grant. They changed the rivalry of two men in Hecht and MacArthur's *The Front Page* to a romantic tangling of a man and a woman and called it *His Girl Friday*. It was even more of a smash at the box office than *Only Angels Have Wings*.

Furthman's analysis of *The Front Page* was simple and concise. "It proves you can write a hit play with an illogical plot. It's about an editor's determination to have his star reporter cover a hanging. Hell, an office boy can cover a hanging. Making it a woman gave it new dimensions. I can do that with a hundred classics."

Author Paul Gallico and I had an unusual affinity. We were look-alikes. When he wore his habitual attire, a black felt hat and black T-shirt, we were easy to tell apart, but when he discarded them for more formal clothes, the similarity between us was striking.

It wasn't unusual for us to be mistaken for each other and one such error occurred during intermission of an opera in Los Angeles.

"This fellow slapped me on the back while we stood at the bar," he reported. "When he said, 'Hello, Sam' I knew he thought I was you."

'Still at MGM?' he asked. I said, 'Yes,' because it was true.

'Didn't know you were an opera fan,' he went on. 'It's quite a surprise seeing you here.'

Meanwhile, Paul continued, the stranger was salaciously eyeing Mrs. Gallico, a very comely lady, but as Paul didn't know who he was talking to, there was no way to introduce them.

The man moved away and Paul summed up the meeting as having beneficial advantages for me.

"Your social standing rose because he saw you at the opera, a high-brow form of entertainment he didn't normally associate with your tastes. He also suspected you were using the opera as a hideaway to cheat with another woman, which also raised you in his estimation because in choosing Pauline Gallico as the other woman in your life you showed impeccable taste. On the whole, you came out very well."

Gallico was writing a series of short stories dealing with a journalist involved with European intrigues and I subsequently bought one called *Assignment: Paris* for Columbia. We were approaching the summer of 1939, and most informed individuals believed war was a certainty. Harry Cohn didn't.

Beatrice Kaufman did.

Dear Sam:
I spend most of my time these days cowering in my comfortable bed with the radio turned on to hear the latest European horror. George is the eternal optimist; no one is

dead to him before the embalmer's visit and I doubt if he thinks Albania has really been turned over to the Italians. And he does not think there is going to be war. But I do, and I am now wishing it would begin so that perhaps in my very old age I can sit by the fireside and think it all over. I shall go to this war, in what capacity I don't know. I made up a dreadful joke about the capacity in which I should like to serve, but I don't know how to write it. Whore de combat, but it's better if you say it.

Your Hellman story came at the perfect moment; I have broken with the left flank, and vice versa.[1] While I was out west Mrs. Parker-Campbell had a charming drunken conversation with George in which, in no uncertain terms, she told him what she thought of him as a writer. George was much too agreeable, and flushed with victory, she turned to Mr. Maugham and delivered a few four-lettered descriptions of his literary style. This has served to loosen the tiny bonds still left of a friendship which I should have abandoned years ago. Lillian, too, I am estranged from, but this has been done without a scene; our interests and points of view are too divergent, although I must say that I admire her as a strong, determined and ruthless woman.

No news of special interest that I know of. The two Rover boys (Kaufman and Moss Hart) are going to work in a week or so—I don't think they know on what, but they will begin a series of loose conversations which they hope to turn into a compact little comedy.[2] They're both in excellent spirits; Moss had managed to spend all of his money, including what he is now getting from RKO for The American Way. *He has moved*

1. Lillian Hellman attended a party given by Samuel Goldwyn for Eleanor Roosevelt. The First Lady had noted in her newspaper column "My Day" that she attended Miss Hellman's play *The Little Foxes* and what she thought about it. Lillian marched up to her and said, "I read that you think my play extremely unpleasant" to which Mrs. Roosevelt replied, "Yes, and it is, isn't it?"
2. These loose conversations resulted in the play *You Can't Take It with You* which won the Pulitzer Prize and was made into a film by Frank Capra for Columbia.

a forest of great trees onto his hillside in the country,[3] *and also*
he has rented a small house in NY way over near the river on
East 57th, which he is busy furnishing in complete Victorian
style . . .

Are you coming East? I wish you would.

It's nine-thirty, and my bed time. We had fourteen for
dinner last night including Lilli Darvas (Molnar's last wife), her
lover, and Baroness Hatvany . . . and I am exhausted by my
social efforts. Love to you, and write again.

Beatrice

Cohn was making plans to spend the summer of 1939 in
Europe. He loved Paris and the Riviera, and planned to stay at
the best hotels, revel in the nightlife and steer clear of the
racetracks and gambling casinos. His disastrous summer of '38
at Saratoga had been an expensive lesson.

My position at Columbia was meaningless without him.
There would be nobody in charge, no one to make decisions.
It was a condition almost universal in the Hollywood studios.
For whatever reason—fear that an underling might usurp
power, or the belief by the boss that he was immortal—many
studios were left rudderless when the top executive was away.

That summer of '39 glowed with announcements of new
plays, new playwrights and new players all through the East
from Maine to Virginia. I suggested that I could line up the
most promising and parade them before him in New York
when he came through there the end of August.

He was seated behind his desk looking as gloomy as I had
ever seen him. Nearby, the bulky frame of Irving Briskin was
slumped in a chair, staring off into space.

"Whatever you're selling, I'm not buying," announced
Cohn.

3. Moss Hart's rearrangement of twelve hundred trees on his Bucks County, Pennsylvania farm elicited the comment attributed to many but actually said by Alexander
Woollcott, "It shows what God could do if He had money."

"You really should listen, Harry," I said.

He waved away any conversation but motioned for me to sit down while he turned his attention to Briskin. I soon gathered that Briskin believed he had a malignant cancer. They were waiting word from his doctor that very moment.

"I'll kill myself," said Briskin. "I'll find a way to do it like that—"

He snapped his fingers the way he did when giving commands to writers, directors and film editors.

"You're gonna be okay," said Cohn. "I'll take you out on the town tonight and we'll celebrate." When Briskin failed to react, he turned to me. "What do you want?"

I explained my plan for a tour of the summer theaters while he was out of the country, but he wasn't listening. Irving Briskin's tragedy overshadowed everything. Then a strident voice came over his intercom from the studio switchboard.

"Here's that call," said the operator.

Briskin shivered and Cohn took a deep breath. He picked up the earpiece so only he would hear the message.

"Yeah?"

When he hung up, he grinned.

"It's benign, you stupid jerk," he said. "The Doc says he told you all along." He stopped because Irving Briskin had begun to weep. Cohn jumped out of his chair, ran to embrace him and they stood together crying in each other's arms.

When they pulled out of it, Cohn thought my going east was a great idea. I could line up actors and actresses and book a studio where we could make tests of them in New York. He would be back from Europe and personally direct the tests the first week in September.

We shipped our car east and arranged to sublet an East Side terrace apartment that belonged to Lillian and Dorothy Gish. It was furnished in delicate good taste, befitting the fragile image of these two early screen stars. To protect some of it, we relegated a number of chairs to a position against a wall and nobody ever sat in them.

The night of the Fourth of July, I sat up late and alone in the swaying observation car of the Twentieth Century Limited, racing from Chicago to New York. The rain was beating down furiously. I was reading a *New York Evening Telegram* which, that night, was black with headlines of crisis in Europe. Hitler had ruled Germany nearly seven years and a new crisis was not uncommon but each one was increasing in intensity.

The current crisis had to do with a corridor through Poland to the Free City of Danzig. It divided Germany from East Prussia. Hitler demanded that Poland give him Danzig and erase the corridor. He offered a nonaggression pact in exchange. Poland refused.

In addition to the Danzig story, the *Telegram* carried an illustrated feature prominently displaying a number of Germans who had fled to the United States. Among a dozen illustrious faces in the photos were Albert Einstein and Thomas Mann.

I was engrossed in these stories when a tall, blond six-footer of some thirty birthdays entered and took a chair directly across from me.

"It is too bad about the rain," he said, in precise English with a German accent. "It will interfere with the fireworks for your Independence Day, no?"

I admitted this was so, but patriotically assured him it did not happen often. I remembered very few Fourth of Julys being rained out. I do not speak to strangers often and care little for smoking-car chatter. But the newcomer was inclined to be talkative.

"Why do your newspapers make so much of this little incident in Europe?" he asked. It was his second use of the word "your" and I asked where he was from. He was Mr. Rudolf of Hamburg, now living in China. He was going to spend four months with his parents in Germany. His dress was impeccably western and one could not have guessed he had spent the last five years in the Orient. But he assured me this was so. In turn, I introduced myself and said I was in the movie business. We chatted amiably until he again downplayed the Danzig crisis.

I told him I thought it was important. "Of course you would think so," he retorted. "It is because of your corrupt American newspapers. All they write about is War! War! War!"

"You don't think there'll be war?" I asked.

He snorted at the suggestion. "Germany is entitled to Danzig! It belonged to us in the fifteenth century!"

"Then the Indians are entitled to all the country we're passing through," I said, pointing out the rain-drenched window. "I may not be 'up' on my history, but if we start putting the world back to the fifteenth century, there'll be a hell of a lot of rearranging to do."

"Hitler is absolutely right about Danzig but your American newspapers never tell truths. It is like their stories of the Jews being badly treated by the Fuhrer!"

"Oh! You agree with Hitler's racial policies?"

"Of course. Germany must protect itself against the Jews and the Communists. Since the first World War they have tried to destroy Germany. Why don't you Hollywood people show the truth? Make your films show Hitler as he really is and all the good he does for the world!"

I picked up the feature article about Einstein and Mann and almost flung it in his face.

"America is lucky. Thanks to Hitler we have these men over here now. And you can take one thought back to Germany with you. There'll be a war and the U.S.A. will be in it and if you stay there four months you'll be damn lucky to get out alive!"

I slammed the door of the observation car and when I entered our compartment, Marie said, "You're as white as a sheet. What happened to you?"

I told her I had just met my first Nazi.

My blood pressure must have been astronomical, and world events would prove I also reached some fair heights of prophecy. But apparently, my outburst had little impact on Mr. Rudolph. Next morning, on the platform at Grand Central

Station, he was following a porter loaded down with magnificent matching luggage. He wore a stylish camel's hair overcoat and a derby hat. He came and stood before me.

"Remember," he said, "it is as I told you. There will be no war!"

He clicked his heels like a Prussian army officer, tipped his hat and bowed to Marie, then hurried after the porter.

Soon after my arrival in New York, Sinclair Lewis made a date to go to Hoboken for an evening of bier-stube entertainment. It would be my first talent-seeking safari on behalf of Harry Cohn.

Casual readers often confused Sinclair Lewis and Upton Sinclair. The novels of both writers dealt with social evils and political conditions. They made Upton Sinclair something of an outcast but did the opposite for Sinclair Lewis.

Despite an unpleasant skin ailment which gave him the appearance of peeling after a bad sunburn (quite upsetting to squeamish dinner companions) Hollywood hostesses fought for the honor of having Sinclair Lewis to dinner.

An easy conversationalist, he honored and flattered all women. They called him "Red" even after his locks were a distinct gray. They were long in front and inclined to stray down on his forehead. He was tall and very thin, wiry and active. He was never relaxed.

He was stage-struck. He wanted to act and be friends with actresses, the younger the better. When he sold a book to the studios, which was pretty nearly every time he wrote one, he came to Hollywood whether the contract called for it or not and hung about while the film was in preparation and shooting. Often, he promised the same part to half a dozen starlets.

My principal purchase from him was *It Can't Happen Here*, a rousing fiction of dictatorship in America. It scared the daylights out of a lot of readers, which finally included the top executives of Metro-Goldwyn-Mayer. It scared Louis B. Mayer into shelving the property, at the urging of the timid Motion Picture Producers Association, after Thalberg paid fifty thousand dollars for the rights and more to Sidney Howard for the screenplay.

Howard had dramatized other Lewis material, including *Dodsworth*, for stage and screen. Both were hurt by MGM's unwillingness to film *It Can't Happen Here*. They couldn't understand the lack of backbone in a great organization, when they, as individualists, were willing to risk their necks for their beliefs. The film would credit them as the creators, not some executive who feared the wrath of a Commissar, a Fuhrer or a President.

As proof of their feelings, they related that when the stage rights to *Dodsworth* were sold to a producer in Germany, an affidavit was affixed to the contracts sent them. It demanded they warrant under oath they had no Jewish blood in their veins. The authors dutifully swore to what was required and returned it to Germany, Lewis signing his name "Sinclair Lewisohn" and Howard "Sidney Horowitz." They never heard from the producer again.

On our agreed date, Lewis and I rode the ferry to Hoboken, which had become the "in" place for after-dark entertainment. New Yorkers were drawn by the praise the shows received from writer Christopher Morley, who garnered reams of publicity for the lively Jersey town. It may be presumed as coincidence that Morley was also coproducer of the quaint melodramas being performed—or perhaps better described as over-performed—on the west shore of the Hudson. Sizeable audiences were filling the theatre-bars to overflowing, exhorted to cheer the lovers and hiss the stalking villain. It was all good clean noise.

Lewis and I were standing in the crowded bar at intermission (the play stopped briefly but the beer drinking didn't), when a belligerent voice suddenly roared above the chatter and we discovered it was aimed in our direction.

I had known Ward Morehouse, critic and occasional playwright, many years before, on Broadway. I had no recollection of ever offending him, but here he was, fists clenched, proclaiming that Lewis and I were the world's greatest sons-of-bitches and he intended to finish us off for the good of all humanity.

The crowd parted to let him make good on it, and Ward launched himself at us from across the lobby like a yapping terrier. He was sloshed with alcohol. In fact I once heard him referred to as "Alcoholic Ward," and this attack on us was made doubly ludicrous by his personal physique, which may be politely described as diminutive. Lewis and I, both six-feet tall, towered over him.

We had no problem avoiding his rush. We simply stepped aside and he went flying by and crashed into a wall. He turned and regrouped his pugilistic attitude, then made ready for a second take-off, madder than ever. The watching crowd, knowing nothing about any of us, cheered him on.

Lewis bent close to my ear. "If we lay a hand on this shrimp we'll be marked 'villains'," he whispered tensely. "This crowd will lynch us!"

"What do you suggest?" I whispered back.

"Flight!"

We ran like cowards, Morehouse screaming after us, daring us to return. We didn't pause. I never saw the second act of *The Black Crook*. Whatever movie talent was in the cast went undiscovered. Next time I saw Morehouse he was his usual friendly self; neither of us mentioned Hoboken.

Strangely, my next venture across the Hudson was also disrupted and incomplete. Columbia's biggest and best star was in New York. Sultry-voiced, shy Jean Arthur expressed a desire to visit a summer theatre and I readily invited her to join me in an evening at the Paper Mill Playhouse in Millburn, New Jersey, where Irene Castle was performing in Noel Coward's *Tonight at 8:30*.

We met for an early dinner at the 21 Club. Jean was a great public favorite, her popularity rocketing upward with a succession of films in which she was the love foil opposite Gary

Cooper, Cary Grant, and Jimmy Stewart. On screen Jean was an aggressive charmer, but in reality her shyness was almost painful. She found it difficult to mix with people.

Inside the 21 Club, Jean had all the privacy she wanted. But when we stepped out to the curb to get into my car, she was surrounded by a horde of autograph seekers, mysteriously alerted to her presence. She pushed through them, refusing to sign any of the books or photographs they thrust at her.

The car window on her side was open, not too surprising for a hot night in a pre-air-conditioning era. She started to wind it closed as I put the motor in gear. Then it turned out that one enterprising young fan had his arm, book and pen inside the window and I had to brake quickly to keep him from losing all of them. Despite his howls that this near-accident deserved Jean's autograph, she would have none of it. As we drove off, the boy shouted that he would never see another of her films and would spread the word to all his friends.

I drove downtown with a quietly depressed movie star at my side. Then we found the tunnel to Jersey jammed with traffic, a solid line of cars stretched for a mile in front of the Manhattan entrance.

"I dare you to pull out and go to the head of the line," she said.

Somewhere between Fifty-second Street and Canal, the usual sparkle had returned to her eyes.

I streaked past a screaming mob of outraged drivers until a substantially-built New York cop rolled out in front of us and stood like an unclimbable palisade in our path.

As he ambled toward us, scowling furiously, Jean leaned out and in her unmistakable screen-husky voice, said, "I made him do it, Mister Officer." He came closer and she reacted.

"Why, officer, I swear you look just like Gary Cooper!"

He, too, reacted. "Jean Arthur! Wow! What a surprise! How about an autograph for my old lady?" Jean poked me in the ribs, grinning. She knew when to sign autographs. She scribbled her name on a scrap of paper, whereupon the cop held up the cars to get us at the front of the line and into the tunnel.

We had seats in the front row at the Paper Mill and at intermission a swarm of playgoers rushed down the aisle with outstretched pens and programs.

While she signed the first of these, others recognized her and the requests grew in number. Almost the whole audience lined up. She murmured, "Let's get out of here," and I never saw the second act of *Tonight at 8:30* either.

I was proving to myself that nothing could kill man's love for entertainment. The pastoral playhouses I attended all had one thing in common—they made pleasure as tough as possible for their customers. Benches were hard, backless, and unrelentingly uncomfortable. Theatres were invariably off the main roads, there were not enough directional arrows, posters that could announce the current play were neglected, the title of last week's show was prominent and next week's invisible.

Three summer theatre managers dropped with heart attacks during the early weeks of the season, several directors walked out when unable to cope with established stars who said they would work but preferred to vacation. Despite these malfunctions, most of the rustic showplaces did sell-out business. That spoke volumes for the lure of theatre. Or, if one preferred a more cynical point of view, the healthy business in these barns was due to the boredom of city folk marooned in the country after dark.

The Red Barn at Locust Valley was built directly alongside the Long Island Railroad tracks. Soon after the curtains parted, the 9:03 roared through, not only drowning out the author's words but scaring the daylights out of the audience. It happened again when a heavy freight practically dashed across the stage during a tense moment of the play's climax.

At Milton-on-the-Hudson trains approached the performance from a valley. They could be heard puffing uphill for an interminable time while the actors froze and stood as immobile statues until the lingering chug-chug-chug drifted away. Then, as though touched by a magician's wand, they all came to life again.

The opening night of *The Grass Is Always Greener* was performed at Surrey, Maine, in fog so heavy it got into the theatre barn and obstructed the view of the actors from the audience.

Summer enthusiasms, blistering heat and vacationing playgoers helped create fantasies that a poor play was a good one. Many producers learned that a triumphant try-out in a barn didn't guarantee a White Way wow. When a production bombed on Broadway its producer wondered what had happened to his brain. The summer theatres provided a curious phenomenon, for August audiences loved a play in spite of the rumble of a passing freight, while October audiences disliked the same play because someone coughed.

Experienced actors, knowing Broadway would be deadly dull in the heat, found a pleasant form of minstrelsy in the summer theatres. Dedicated troupers accepted weeks of study and rehearsals of unworthy plays, poor quarters and, in many cases, no money. They were spending the time living their beloved theatre.

This fascination was apparent in William Castle's troupe at Stony Creek, Connecticut. Performers and their families, their children, and their pets lived together in a ramshackle, decaying hotel on Long Island Sound with a huge unpainted veranda. This weather-beaten hostelry, the Flying Point Hotel, was reported to have been most fashionable and exclusive— in the nineties! In 1939 it seemed centuries behind the times, and everything, from ancient gas fixtures to the insufficient plumbing, creaked with long-gone grandeur. But the halls echoed laughter and song, while dramatic lines were declaimed aloud on the beach in front of the hotel by actors in bathing suits. They were true thespians who weren't sure what life held in store for them one moment after September 1 brought down the curtain. Tonight they would be on stage and today they were happy because of it. Indeed, in that great wooden ghost of past greatness, one might see only one rather sad and pensive figure. That would be me.

I spent part of an evening watching an earnest bevy of apprentice actresses perform *Little Women* at Peterborough, New Hampshire. The other part of the evening was spent with the rest of the audience ducking the bats power-diving into our faces throughout the show.

Many theatres like that one used apprentices in so-called "Schools of the Theatre," which were appended to the main company. These hopefuls paid money for the privilege of their dubious connection with thespia. Many of them never came closer to the footlights than to replace a bulb. They painted scenery, planted posters in local shop windows, ushered audiences to their seats and now and then performed offstage noises.

Some theatres made the girls learn ballet and the boys do physical exercise, and a *Life* magazine layout showed a lawn full of apprentices at Abington, Virginia, studying mass love-making. Regrettably, I never did get down there.

It was the year of *Our Town*. Thornton Wilder's homey drama was everywhere. Half-a-dozen prominent males sat in camp-chairs to the side of the stage, in accord with the playscript, introducing the folksy characters and explaining what made them do what they were doing. Sinclair Lewis and Wilder, himself, appeared in performances of this bland little play from which there was no escape.

Venerable Charley Coburn insisted I see his group of students at the Mohawk Drama Festival in upstate New York. It would be to witness the inevitable *Our Town*, part of the summer session at Union College, Schenectady.

Coburn was one of the great character actors of his time, a friend and opponent in the Hoyle Club, a fanatical group of poker players who met in high-stakes weekly sessions all year round. Also known, whimsically, as the Thanatopsis Marching and Chowder Club, its members were writers, actors and directors and because of the extensive traveling required in their calling, the club held sessions on both coasts. It would be expensive recreation, but after a week of typical try-out turkeys, or the suffering of another *Our Town*, I always tried to get back to the city on the night of the game, the fun of it rendering my losses less painful.

The New York Chapter held its get-togethers upstairs at the Barberry Room, a quiet bistro on East Fifty-second Street. It was a strictly no-nonsense contest, but the cards were mixed with jokes, gossip, food and drink and show business talk.

George S. Kaufman, in spite of his reputation for dry wit and terse one-liners, played poker with frowning demeanor and silent concentration. He had a low tolerance of irrelevant matters, contending they were useful only if women were seated at the table, a notion totally abhorrent to him. "I know other games in which women are indispensable," he said when actress Constance Bennett tried to join the club, "but not cards."

The end of each session was signaled by the light of dawn, which traditionally heralded a final round, played in tribute to "Crouse's Grandmother." Nobody present, including playwright Russell Crouse, knew anything about her but it was considered a mark of respect to a wonderful old lady. Keyed-up losers often stretched the game through another round into the morning, all the extra playing dedicated to the playwright's family heritage back into antiquity.

Crouse and Howard Lindsay, another Hoyle Club player, were finishing their new play, a dramatization of a series of *New Yorker* magazine stories. *Life with Father* would soon try out in Skowhegan, Maine. The theatre was booked, the casting all set except for the title role, for which they hoped to secure Walter Huston. I planned to drive on to Maine following my visit to Coburn's group and see the show on its opening night.

In addition to his many triumphs in theatre and films, Charley Coburn also achieved a few at cards.

Once, in a stud game when the hour was late, his head drooped, his eyes closed, he languorously turned over an upturned ace and began to breathe the sonorous sounds of the dead tired.

Prodded awake, Charley begged to be allowed to sleep but was forced to abide by a club rule that the first ace must bet. Swearing, sighing, casting hopeful glances at a nearby couch, he was made to bet each card dealt him. He would nod into sleep and again be roused and have to chip along as the players engaged in a lively duel with high raises. It was presumed that he turned over his ace because his hole card was a poor match. However, at the showdown, Charley had aces back-to-back and beaming radiantly, fully awake, he called the attention of the unappreciative losers to his performance while he raked in a tableful of blue chips.

He also loved the trotting races, a popular sport on the Chatauqua Circuit upstate, so his days were as full and rich as his nights.

As Dean of the Players Club in Gramercy Square, he enticed many members to Mohawk and one of them, Frank Craven, was starring in *Our Town* when I attended.

Saturday morning the students assembled under the campus elms for an informal lecture by the star of the week, followed by a question and answer period. In his opening moments, Craven delivered a broadside against Hollywood (which had never broken down doors to acquire his services) and a bitter crack about "Jewish reaction" against *Our Town*. He alienated me on these two counts and I planned to ask him, during the questioning, if he knew that Jed Harris had produced the original Broadway production.

But the gathering of eager young tyros of the theatre gave me no chance. They plied him with questions about how they could make their way in the profession and to all of them, Craven told them to forget it, choose some other way of life.

However they were not easily deterred.

"Tell us how you got started," pleaded one.

"I was lucky," parried the actor.

"How do you get lucky?"

It was no easy question to answer and Craven never replied to it, being saved by the bell. A deep-pealing instrument in the school tower announced it was noon. Craven verified the time on his wristwatch, said he was late for a golf date and sauntered away.

Many stars were touring the summer circuit in plays of their own selection, being booked to perform with the resident company. Those local actors rehearsed without the star.

Edward Everett Horton was such a star. His play was a light bit of summer froth, *Springtime for Henry*. Horton carried a full company with him through New England and its neighboring states. Somehow, this method of packaging the complete cast was not reported ahead to Clinton, New York, where the barnstormers valiantly rehearsed the play in anticipation of Mr. Horton joining them. Consternation was complete when the star appeared with an entire company and had no need of an extra set of actors.

The truly professional companies were on Cape Cod, Massachusetts, in Bucks County, Pennsylvania, at Westport, Connecticut, and in Skowhegan, Maine. At the latter, the best new play of the year made its appearance.

There was no doubt that *Life with Father* would be a hit in New York. Its magic was apparent in the first few moments. Unable to land Walter Huston for the lead, the play was having its tryout with its coauthor, Howard Lindsay, performing in the title part. Everything about it clicked; it was no short-lived summer blossom.

Actor Keenan Wynn and his wife Evie occupied a rustic bungalow on the theatre grounds and after the premiere, Marie and I joined the party there. Lindsay, with his wife Dorothy Stickney as Mother, had come across superbly. It seemed they had no need to look further for players. But they weren't sure.

Casting was the only thing they weren't sure about. Coauthors Lindsay and Crouse and producer Oscar Serlin were sure they had a Broadway hit and were negotiating for the prestigious Empire Theatre. The enthralled audience in Skowhegan had rushed to the box office after the first performance to buy seats for their friends and to see it again themselves.

At Keenan Wynn's opening-night party, casting problems finally ground to a no-decision halt, at which point I proposed they sell the film rights to Columbia Pictures.

In a tense world, teetering between peace and war, this nostalgic, bittersweet comedy seemed just what was needed to escape the poisons in the air. I took a chance and offered to write a check for a hundred thousand dollars. I guaranteed Harry Cohn would make it good; inwardly I prayed he would. I never discovered how this gamble might have come off; my offer was turned down.

With ten days left to assemble the young players I had picked and prepare the test facilities, we raced for New York, stopping at Ogunquit, Maine, to see Sinclair Lewis in *Our Town*. Completely stage-struck, the novelist said he was through with books. He planned to devote his life to the theatre. Part of the attraction, it seemed, was the plentitude of adoring actresses. He had written a new play, *Angela Is 22*, which he was certain would draw a virtual harem of ingenues to him.

His companion in Ogunquit was a vivid young sophisticate, eighteen-year-old Diana, daughter of John Barrymore. She was as spirited and vivacious as her father. I offered her a test but she professed a vast disinterest in films. Some day, she said, she might think about the movies but now, drink in hand, a famous author by her side, she was too comfortable to embrace the uncertain beckonings of Hollywood. Lewis, grinning like a satyr, agreed with her and subtly influenced her decision.

When we reached the city, Marie arranged to leave at once for California and our two boys. There had been many such separations, the penalty of an unending search for writers and stories.

This one marked the end of our tenth summer since I announced we were going west on that New Year's Eve in New York. A little sadder than usual, I carried her bags onto the platform at Grand Central Station and we embraced until the train carried her out of my sight.

I walked uptown reflecting how she had contributed so much to the joy of those years. Every turn of career, every vicissitude, every decision was made easier by her unhesitating support and her sharing of my feelings for this great gaudy spree we had known.

She let me know about it in a roundabout way. It had to do with the man in her life before I met her. Her affection was all too apparent, she made no secret of it. For him, her eyes would cloud with a faraway look and try though she might to repress them, sobs escaped from her lips.

But he was dead, the victim of a sudden, violent death. Her memories disturbed the first months we knew each other but the pall they cast over our relationship finally disappeared. Until this summer of 1939 when, rather shyly and without explanation, she asked that I go with her to a street on the outskirts of the city. There she gazed thoughtfully at a busy intersection and I realized it was the place where he died. Then, with her eyes shining, she put her arms around me and said, "I know now that what happened here brought me the happiest moments of my life."

Because Columbia was minor among major studios, with a small acting company, I held the selection of summer aspirants down to a half-dozen boys and girls. Arrangements for the tests were set up at the Fox Film Company's studio in midtown Manhattan, on the west side.

There were two usual screen tests. One measured aspirants for a role in a movie about to be made. For them, the test scene was from the actual screenplay, giving the player the character he or she would be called on to portray in the production.

The second type was for tyros, aimed at winning them a studio contract. It was Hollywood's custom to test samples of their talents in a scene from some previously produced film. These studio-prepared test scenes were in constant use and they grew boringly familiar to studio executives who passed judgment on them. The tyros suffered by comparison to the properly costumed, carefully directed and professionally acted player already seen in the movies they strove to emulate. It wasn't easy for an amateur to do better than Jean Arthur or outshine Gary Cooper, with none of the production grandeur included in the test.

Instead of following that customary path, I chose the test material from Dorothy Parker's short stories, Ernest Hemingway's novels, and some cultured splendor of Evelyn Waugh.

All the youngsters were to be in New York three days after Labor Day, giving them time to get to the city after the traditional conclusion of a summer season.

However, Cohn arrived before the holiday and, chafed with the boredom he had experienced on shipboard, was annoyed that he had to wait for them. No amount of explanation sufficed, his awareness quotient was nil. It didn't matter at all to him that these young people had given their summer to their theatres and it would be indecent of them to quit, even a day or two before the season's end. But Cohn's impatience was monumental, and after a great deal of telephoning to Pennsylvania and Maine, all agreed to be in New York by Saturday, September 2, the eve of the holiday, when Cohn was to direct their tests.

Friday, September 1, Germany marched into Poland. Saturday, in an atmosphere edgy enough without needing such martial overtones, the group assembled. Actors, cameraman and sound crew were on hand before 9:00 A.M. Director Cohn wasn't.

The crews played cards, smoked, read funny papers. The actors paced the floor in make-up and wardrobe, drinking coffee, mumbling lines, pretending they weren't nervous.

Cohn strode in after eleven with Victor Orsatti, the Hollywood agent who toured Europe with him. They inspected the waiting group of anxious actors, and admitted the three girls looked good.

"Who's first?" asked Cohn.

A bouncy Italian boy jumped into the set and signaled his partner to take her position for the scene. Cohn said, "Lights! Camera! Action!" in traditional Hollywood style.

He made the tests without any rehearsal. Unfamiliar with the scenes, he never knew when they finished. "Why in hell aren't they doing the usual crap?" he asked.

Lacking direction, the boys and girls floundered through extemporaneous movements and stage business they made up as they went along. Often, the cameraman turned his focus one way as they moved in another, completely out of camera range. When the actors reached the end of the mini-scenes and were out of dialogue, they turned helplessly to Cohn. He would call "Cut!" and the camera stopped turning, the lights dimmed and Cohn would say "Print it" and signal the next one.

He ran through the tests in less than an hour. He was quite pleased. He turned to his agent-friend and said, "Hey, Vic, we can make the first race after all." They marched out of the studio without another word to anyone and I tried to explain to the bewildered boys and girls he wasn't always so brusque, so rude, so insensitive. But of course, he was.

That night the Hoyle Club was to convene with the intention of playing poker right through the Labor Day holiday. It could be a dream place for forgetting a nightmare.

A different kind of nightmare was gripping the world overseas, for this Labor Day was more than just an American holiday. Most citizens of Europe, along with others around the world, were holding their breath, and with good reason. One week before, on August 23, Hitler and Stalin signed a nonaggression pact. The fusion of Fascism and Communism caught political thinkers completely by surprise, especially the Hollywood writers who leaned far right or far left. The chaos and confusion and puzzled loyalties that churned through their minds at this unforeseen event were creating turmoil in their ranks, but being three thousand miles east at the time, I was neither involved nor caught in the middle.

A distinguished company of poker players met in the Barberry Room. Crouse and Lindsay were back in town, preparing *Life with Father* for the Empire Theatre. George S. Kaufman said he was looking forward to nonstop winning for two days. He was seconded by Jack Goodman, a popular playboy, the literary editor at Simon and Schuster.

I knew two of the other players only by journalistic reputations. Sportswriter John Kieran had an extraordinary knowledge of foreign history and domestic trivia. Dark-eyed Franklin P. Adams, perpetually scowling, was famous as FPA, editor of "The Conning Tower" which appeared daily opposite the editorial page of the *Herald Tribune*. Poets, wits and raconteurs took enormous pride contributing their inspirations. Seeing their names and offerings in FPA's "Conning Tower" was more important among New York's literati than money, for none was paid.

Money was important to Adams, however. Some years before, I negotiated with him for his services as a screen writer, a form of endeavor with which he had absolutely no experience. I offered him a six-month contract at five hundred dollars a week that he refused, saying, "How come Sidney Howard gets three thousand?"

Playwright Marc Connelly was a jolly, bombastic fellow whose hit play, *Green Pastures*, revealed the erudite thinking beneath his constant, booming laugh. At the game, he assumed a character he called Banker Brown. The Banker's creed was "Nobody goes broke taking a profit" and at times he left shortly after he arrived when he won the early pots. Connelly was indifferent to complaints against these unfriendly actions. They didn't add to his popularity with the players, but his unpopularity on this particular night was for a different reason.

He brought with him a large, early-model portable radio, so early, in fact, that Kaufman claimed it predated Marconi who invented it. Connelly and I had neighboring chairs and he placed the box on the floor between us.

It emitted unbearably tinny sounds with a grating rasp that further irritated the other players, but he kept it on and he and I strained our ears to keep up with the news. Trying to hear the events in Europe, he turned up the volume whenever the broadcast switched to overseas reports. Then, static of the outer spheres of space added greater cacophony. Shrugging off the fury of our fellow card players, Connelly kept the radio tuned in. It continued to deliver news of doom, as German hordes crossed the borders of Poland. Stuka planes were dive-bombing defenseless civilians from the air and Swastika-marked tanks gunned them from the ground. Proclaiming the greatness of his thousand-year Reich, Hitler was screaming defiance to the world. At this poker game, only Connelly and I were listening.

The radio suddenly switched to London and through the decrepit tubes emerged the dolorous voice of England's Prime Minister Chamberlain. Amid the howling of the machine and the poker players we were able to hear the words, "And so we are at war with Germany . . . !"

"Shut that damn thing off and play poker," commanded Adams. Kaufman threatened to call the restaurant manager and have us evicted. When we tried to convey to them what had just occurred in Europe, our highly literate companions expressed a sublime disinterest. Thereupon, Connelly snapped off the offending squawks and we settled down to a serious session of card playing on what had to be one of the most momentous nights of our lives.

World War II had begun.

The gaudy spree was over.

Index

Hurst, Fannie, 155, 156, 166
Huston, Walter, 200, 202
Hyman, Bernie, 21, 23, 26, 38, 39, 40, 41, 94, 132

Ince, Thomas H., 27
Ince Studio, 27
It Can't Happen Here, 193–194

Janis, Elsie, 45
Jazz Singer, The, 19
Johnston, Alva, 148
Johnston, Julanne, 100–101
Jolson, Al, 19
Jordan, Robert, 154
Joyce, Peggy Hopkins, 54

Kahn, Otto H., 53–54
Kalmar, Bert, 125
Kaufman, Beatrice, 155–156, 158, 166, 187
Kaufman, George S., 43, 81, 97, 113, 123–125, 162, 200, 207
Keeler, Ruby, 50
Kellogg, Virginia, 153–154
Kelly, George, 46
Kern, Jerome, 89
Kieran, John, 207
Kingsley, Sidney, 149, 155, 158
Kipling, Rudyard, 43
Knopf, Edwin, 141
Kober, Arthur, 36, 149–151
Kobler, A. J., 111–112

Kohlmar, Freddy, 147–148, 160, 168
Korda, Alexander, 148
Krasna, Norman, 125
Kreuger, Ivar, 78
Kurnitz, Harry, 163

LaCava, Gregory, 172
LaHiff, Billy, 3
Lait, Jack, 4
Lamour, Dorothy, 145
Lederer, Charley, 82, 83, 95, 97–101, 104, 105, 116, 117–118
Leonard, Robert Z., 138
Levant, Oscar, 165
Lewin, Albert, 127, 128, 133
Lewis, Sinclair, 139, 144, 193–195, 203
Lewton, Nina, 34
Life with Father, 202
Lindsay, Howard, 200, 202, 207
Lloyd, Frank, 127
Loew, Marcus, 74
Loos, Anita, 22, 66–67, 155, 161
Loy, Myrna, 102, 104, 119, 132
Lullaby, 58–62

MacArthur, Charlie, 22, 51–55, 58–59, 60–62, 67, 85, 105, 120
McCarthy, Charley, 169
McCrae, Joel, 143

Show business movies,
49–50
Shumlin, Herman, 36, 37
Silberberg, Mendel, 175
Silver Slipper, 8
Sinclair, Upton, 67–72, 115,
116, 193
*Sin of Madelon Claudet,
The,* 62
Sistrom, Joseph, 183–184
Slesinger, Tess, 177
Smith, Madeline, 120
Smith, Walton Hall, 94
Speakeasies, 8, 68
Spence, Ralph, 22
Spewack, Bella, 127,
181–182
Spewack, Sam, 127, 181
Spiegelglass, Leonard, 92
Stallings, Laurence, 22, 155
Stewart, Donald Ogden, 45,
67, 155
Stewart, Jimmy, 196
Stickney, Dorothy, 202
Strictly Dishonorable, 7
Stromberg, Hunt, 21, 27,
120, 132
Strunk, William, 133–134
Sturges, Preston, 7
Summer theatres, 197–202

Tale of Two Cities, A, 123
Taradash, Daniel, 182
Tarzan, The Ape Man
(Burroughs) 41, 42
Taylor, Robert, 118
Thalberg, Irving, 5, 14,
21–22, 26, 33, 35,
45–46, 53, 56, 57, 58,
65, 66, 68, 69, 71–72,
75–76, 85, 86, 95–96,
101–102, 104–105,
112–113, 114, 122, 125,
126, 127, 138–139
  death of, 139
  heart attack of, 86
Thau, Ben, 15, 88
Thaw, Harry K., 16
Thin Man, The, 119
This Side of Paradise
(Fitzgerald), 38, 65
Thomas, Olive, 11
Thorndyke, Pamela, 117,
118
Tibbett, Lawrence, 50
Tracy, Spencer, 132
Trader Horn, 38–42, 77
Transatlantic Flight, 156,
162
Turner, Lana, 177
Twentieth Century, 54–55,
61
20th Century-Fox, 173

Unger, Gladys, 45
Unholy Garden, The, 51,
54, 55, 58, 61

Vajda, Ernest, 88
Van Dusen, William, 156
Van Dyke, Woody, 77
Van Dyke, W. S., 38, 41,
119
Verne, Jules, 136